# INTEGRATING ECOLOGY AND JUSTICE IN A CHANGING CLIMATE

*Edited by*
Sam Mickey

Published by the
*UNIVERSITY OF SAN FRANCISCO PRESS*
Joan and Ralph Lane Center
for Catholic Social Thought and the Ignatian Tradition

University of San Francisco
2130 Fulton Street
San Francisco, CA 94117-1080
www.usfca.edu/lane-center

Collection copyright © 2020
ISBN 978-1-949643-59-6 | paperback
ISBN 978-1-949643-60-2 | epub

Published by the University of San Francisco Press through the Joan and Ralph Lane Center for Catholic Social Thought and the Ignatian Tradition of the University of San Francisco.

The Lane Center Series promotes the center's mission to advance the scholarship and application of the Catholic intellectual tradition in the church and society with an emphasis on social concerns. The series features essays by Lane Center scholars, guest speakers, and USF faculty. It serves as a written archive of Lane Center events and programs and allows the work of the center to reach a broader audience.

# The Lane Center Series

Published by the Joan and Ralph Lane Center for Catholic Social Thought and the Ignatian Tradition at the University of San Francisco, the Lane Center Series explores intersections of faith and social justice. Featuring essays that bridge interdisciplinary research and community engagement, the series serves as a resource for social analysis, theological reflection, and education in the Jesuit tradition.

Visit the Lane Center's website to download each volume and view related resources at www.usfca.edu/lane-center

## Volumes

*A Sukkah in the Shadow of Saint Ignatius:*
*Essays on the History of Jewish-Christian Relations*

*Beyond Borders:*
*Reflections on the Resistance & Resilience Among*
*Immigrant Youth and Families*

*Catholic Identity in Context:*
*Vision and Formation for the Common Good*

*Today I Gave Myself Permission to Dream:*
*Race and Incarceration in America*

*Islam at Jesuit Colleges and Universities*

*Pope Francis and the Future of Catholicism in the United States:*
*The Challenge of Becoming a Church for the Poor*

*The Declaration on Christian Education:*
*Reflections by the Institute for Catholic Education Leadership and the*
*Joan and Ralph Lane Center for Catholic Studies and Social Thought*

*Dorothy Day:*
*A Life and Legacy*

# Table of Contents

# Foreword

ERIN BRIGHAM*

I celebrated my child's first birthday on a foggy December morning in Golden Gate Park. I remember commenting with gratitude that I had taken him to the park nearly every day of his first year on earth. The moderate climate of the Bay Area allowed me to take such luxuries for granted. Two months before his fourth birthday, Northern California faced its worst wildfires in documented history. Before we left the house each day, I would check the air quality index. If it was orange, I would fasten a particle mask over his little face and head to the bus; if it was red, I would fasten him in his car seat and drive; and if it was purple, I kept him home, indoors, all day. The apocalyptic image of my three-year old in a particle mask, dazzled by the color of the smoke-filtered sunlight adds a sense of urgency to address climate change.

This volume emerged out of a roundtable discussion among scholars, activists, and faith leaders responding to the same sense of urgency. Convened by the Joan and Ralph Lane Center for Catholic Social Thought and the Ignatian Tradition in the spring of 2019, we gave particular attention to the role of Jesuit universities in advancing

---

* Erin Brigham, PhD is Executive Director of the Joan and Ralph Lane Center for Catholic Social Thought and the Ignatian Tradition at the University of San Francisco, where she also serves as Chief Mission Officer. She teaches Catholic theology and social thought and her current research focuses on ecclesiology, public theology, and gender in Catholic social thought.

thought and action toward climate justice as a concrete expression of our Jesuit Catholic mission.

Among the top priorities of the International Association of Jesuit Universities (IAJU) is the promotion of environmental and economic justice as interconnected ethical challenges. Contextualizing this priority in conversation with Pope Francis's encyclical, *Laudato si'*, Michael Garanzini, S.J. states, "By linking the environmental crisis to its roots in economic forces, and calling for an integral environmental humanism, the Church has pointed to economic, social, political and psychological changes that are necessary if we are to survive in our "common home". How can all of our institutions take a leadership role in addressing these two challenges, which amount to different sides of the same coin?" [1]

The essays in this volume demonstrate through diverse frames of analysis, the central theme of *Laudato si'*—everything is interconnected. Economic systems and cultural attitudes that marginalize and dehumanize are also driving the exploitation of the earth. From diverse perspectives, the authors in this volume reinforce Pope Francis's challenge to live into an intergenerational solidarity that builds up the common good of our common home.

Jesuit institutions cannot ignore this imperative. The care for our common home has been articulated as one of four Universal Apostolic Preferences (UAPs) that will guide the goals and actions of Jesuit works across the globe. This preference unifies the other UAPs: Finding God through the Spiritual Exercises and Discernment, Journeying with Youth Toward a Hope-Filled Future, and Walking with the Marginalized. Cultivating depth and freedom through an interior life frees us from the idolatry of money and consumption. Walking with the marginalized who are most impacted by the devastating effects of climate change compels us to reimagine an economy that excludes and exploits so many.

---

[1]    A Position Paper from the Task Force on Environmental & Economic Justice For the Delegates of the Society of Jesus, Higher Education Directorate 2018 Meeting in Bilbao, Spain. Available at http://iaju.org

Finally, journeying with youth toward a hope-filled future will teach us the way to care for our common home. When I think of my child whose reality will continue to be marked by periods of toxic air and extreme weather, it is easy to become discouraged. But I am inspired by Greta Thunberg and other young activists calling us back to the urgency of this moment. Those of us in higher education occupy a privileged place to listen to youth as they name the signs of the times and call us to action.

# Introduction

SAM MICKEY*

Humankind is currently facing unprecedented environmental and economic challenges. Poverty, pollution, homelessness, epidemics, habitat destruction, species extinction, and climate change are among a seemingly endless litany of critical problems that are spread across the planet. Moreover, those problems appear to be intensifying, making matters increasingly urgent. The way that people respond to the mounting challenges of this historical moment is a matter of human survival, but it is not only that. Rather, as the present volume makes clear, it is also a matter of justice.

Concern for justice has found expression in various ways across cultures throughout history. Ideals of fairness, righteousness, reciprocity, and equality are encoded in many laws, ethical norms, and religious traditions. Indeed, a sense of justice seems to extend throughout much of the animal kingdom. Animal behavior scientists describe values of cooperation, empathy, fair play, and justice at work not only in humans, and not only in other primates, but in various species of mammals, birds, invertebrates, fish, reptiles, and

---

* Sam Mickey is an Adjunct Professor of Theology and Religious Studies at the University of San Francisco. He is a consultant for the Forum on Religion and Ecology at Yale, and the Reviews Editor for the journal *Worldviews: Global Religions, Culture, and Ecology*. His work focuses on integrating philosophical, religious, and scientific perspectives on human-Earth relations.

amphibians.[1] Even aside from the ways that nonhuman animals exhibit their own orientations toward justice, the natural world is integral to justice. Justice has material conditions, which are inseparable from the natural environment. The pursuit of clean air, habitable land, nutritious food, and clean freshwater is fundamental to the pursuit of justice.

Environmental degradation and destruction are not merely physical phenomena. They involve cultural and spiritual values. Losing access to the wondrous splendor of the wild is a spiritual loss. The American novelist and environmentalist Wallace Stegner described this spiritual loss in his famous "Wilderness Letter"—a letter written in 1960 pleading for the preservation of wilderness.

> Something will have gone out of us as a people if we ever let the remaining wilderness be destroyed; if we permit the last virgin forests to be turned into comic books and plastic cigarette cases; if we drive the few remaining members of the wild species into zoos or to extinction; if we pollute the last clear air and dirty the last clean streams and push our paved roads through the last of the silence [...] We need to demonstrate our acceptance of the natural world, including ourselves; we need the spiritual refreshment that being natural can produce. And one of the best places for us to get that is in the wilderness where the fun houses, the bulldozers, and the pavement of our civilization are shut out.[2]

In the decades since Stegner wrote that letter, environmental destruction has intensified dramatically, and what he saw as a "geography of hope" has become increasingly hopeless.[3] Unsustainable and unjust economic growth is having ecological impacts at a planetary scale, as evidenced by the emergency of anthropogenic climate change. It is

---

[1]  Marc Bekoff, *Animal Passions and Beastly Virtues: Reflections on Redecorating Nature* (Philadelphia: Temple University Press, 2006); Marc Bekoff and Jessica Pierce, *Wild Justice: The Moral Lives of Animals* (Chicago: University of Chicago Press, 2009).

[2]  Wallace Stegner, *The Sound of Mountain Water: The Changing American West* (New York: Vintage Books, 1997), 140-143.

[3]  Ibid, 147.

this dire situation that Pope Francis addresses in his 2015 encyclical, *Lauadto si'*.

According to Francis, hope is not lost. "All it takes is one good person to restore hope!"[4] In the Bible, this is exemplified in the story of Noah, "who remained innocent and just" in a time when humankind's presence on Earth was dominated by wickedness. In the same way that God opened a way to a new beginning for humankind through Noah, a new beginning remains possible for humankind today. The Pope's encyclical expresses a restoration of hope in a time of ecological emergency. Today, the challenge of remaining just is a challenge of tending not only to the poor, marginalized, and destitute, but also to the interconnected life, land, air, and water of Earth. The cry for justice today is *"both the cry of the earth and the cry of the poor."*[5] This means that justice takes place at the intersection of ecology and economy. The "eco" shared by economy and ecology derives from the Greek *oikos*, meaning "home" or "dwelling." In that sense, justice is given an apt formulation in the subtitle of *Laudato si': On Care for Our Common Home*. In other words, *Laudato si'* is about caring for the world in a time of climate crisis.[6]

Caring for our common home requires the integration of many fields of study and multiple ways of knowing, from cultures and religious traditions, from economists and policymakers, and from ecology and other areas of environmental science. This interdisciplinary approach is what Pope Francis calls "integral ecology." More than an idea or a theory, integral ecology is a way of life. Accordingly, it involves more than information and data, and more than the scientific method. It involves a transformation of one's very being. It is a conversion experience. This conversion is not a religious conversion. Rather,

---

4    Pope Francis, *Laudato si': On Care for Our Common Home* (Vatican City: Libreria Editrice Vaticana, 2015), 9.

5    Ibid, 35.

6    Frank Pasquale, ed., *Care for the World: Laudato si' and Catholic Social Thought in an Era of Climate Crisis* (New York: Cambridge University Press, 2019).

it is an "ecological conversion."[7] The Pope is not asking people to abandon whatever religious affiliation they might currently have. He is inviting Catholics and, indeed, "every person living on this planet," to include ecology within your current context, to bring a sense of interconnectedness into your personal lives and into our communities and institutions.[8]

The interconnectedness of human-Earth relations invites joyous participation, celebration, and gratitude, yet it is wrought with suffering, and there is precious little time to carry out a transition away from an unsustainable civilization predicated on rampant injustice and toward peaceful, just, and regenerative ways of being in the world. The challenge is far greater than finding sustainable ways to grow and develop. More than that, the very ideas of growth and development must be critically analyzed and rethought. The predominant model of economic growth in recent decades has been profoundly harmful, both socially and environmentally. Accordingly, degrowth is arguably an important strategy for integral ecology.[9] From the standpoint of ecological conversion, simple and humble lifestyles are more appropriate than endless busyness and the demand for ever-increasing productivity. The chapters that follow articulate some of the details of these kinds of lifestyle changes, cultural shifts, and socioeconomic transitions.

The present volume takes up the joyous yet daunting challenge of caring for our common home and seeking justice in an interconnected world. As Erin Brigham mentions in the Foreword to this collection, each of the contributors came together for a roundtable discussion at the University of San Francisco in the spring of 2019, hosted by the Joan and Ralph Lane Center for Catholic Social Thought and the Ignatian Tradition. Other attendees included scholars, community members, activists, faith leaders, and farmers, whose perspectives

---

[7]    Pope Francis, *Laudato si'*, 140.
[8]    Ibid, 4.
[9]    Roberto Puggioni, "Pope Francis and Degrowth: A Possible Dialogue for a Post-Capitalist Alternative, *International Journal of Public Theology* 11.1 (2017).

led to interesting and enriching dialogue about the theoretical and practical questions involved with the integration of environmental and economic justice in a changing climate. The contributors to this book (including myself) offer these chapters as a representation of the main ideas and concerns circulating in discussions from that day, and to provide some orientation and grounding to support works of justice within and beyond Jesuit universities.

Following this introduction, there are four chapters. In the first chapter, Vijaya Nagarajan introduces and elaborates on the work of the French cultural critic, historian, and Catholic priest Ivan Illich (1926-2002), whose thinking has been widely influential for scholars and activists engaging with complex problems across many facets of modern society, including education, literacy, transportation, energy use, technological progress, and economic development. Presenting multiple, intersecting paths to environmental and economic justice, Nagarajan considers how Illich's vision of an equitable society resonates with the ecological perspective of Pope Francis as well as the simple, nonviolent ways of life cultivated by Henry David Thoreau and Mahatma Gandhi.

In the next chapter, Sam Mickey draws further attention to the integral ecology of Pope Francis, showing how the ideas expressed in *Laudato si'* draw on two of the most prominent ecological thinkers to emerge from Catholicism in the twentieth century: the liberation theologian Leonardo Boff (b. 1938) and the cultural historian and Passionist priest Thomas Berry (1914-2009). The connections between Pope Francis and the works of Boff and Berry indicate the global, multicultural scope of integral ecology as well as the radical ethical and political practices that emerge with ecological conversion. An indication of the characteristics of such practices is outlined in the next chapter, in which Adrienne Johnson and Brian Dowd-Uribe analyze the role of degrowth in agriculture.

In contrast to the predominant discourses on degrowth, which tend to focus on the developed countries of the Global North, Johnson and Dowd-Uribe draw attention to the ecological, historical, and political dynamics of the Global South, considering specific examples from agriculture in Costa Rica and Ecuador. By accounting for differences and links between degrowth in the Global North and Global South, this chapter provides a shared vision for more just forms of agriculture, characterized by small-scale, farmer-friendly, localized food production. Johnson and Dowd-Uribe point the way for degrowth scholars to attend to the cries of colonial and racial injustice across our common home.

In the way that degrowth can bring agriculture back to its local place, the final chapter likewise finds environmental and economic justice in place, as Gerard Kuperus connects the integral principles of *Laudato si'* with the work of Dōgen Zenji, the thirteenth century founder of the Sōtō school of Zen Buddhism. For Dōgen, Buddhist practice is a way of connecting with "mountains and rivers," which is to say, a way of realizing one's immersion in the dynamics of the natural world. Kuperus describes the insights of Dōgen by elaborating on the ecological vision of a contemporary Zen practitioner and poet, Gary Snyder (b. 1930), who has been a leading figure for spiritual and political perspectives on ecology in recent decades. Whereas Johnson and Dowd-Uribe brought an integrative perspective to North-South relations, Kuperus facilitates integration along an East-West axis, which resonates with Nagarajan's considerations of Gandhi in connection with Ivan Illich.

All the contributions in this volume indicate that global environmental and economic issues cannot be solved like engineering projects. Something more is required, something that reconnects humans to their embodiment and embeddedness in place, something that recuperates the intimate intertwining of humans with one another and with the myriad creatures of Earth, something that returns humankind to its nonhuman kin: in short, ecological conversion. This volume can be read as a call for ecological conversion, that is, a call that joins the cries of the poor and of the planet in seeking justice and peace for our common home.

# Ivan Illich, the History of Needs, and the Climate Commons

VIJAYA NAGARAJAN*

In this essay, I propose to explore how Ivan Illich, a Catholic priest, social historian, and cultural critic, from the 1950s through the 1990s, investigated the rich history of needs and its relationship to industrially constructed desires. The questions I seek to understand are the following: How does the history of needs relate to climate

*    Vijaya Nagarajan is Associate Professor of Theology/Religious Studies and Environmental Studies at the University of San Francisco. She is the author of *Feeding A Thousand Souls: Women, Ritual and Ecology in India, An Exploration of the Kolam* (Oxford University Press 2019) and many other articles. Her current teaching and research explores the spiritual autobiographies of place, Hinduism and Climate, recovering the multiple languages of the commons, Ivan Illich, energy and equity, South Asia, and California. I wish to thank Dr. Erin Brigham, Executive Director, Joan and Ralph Lane Center for Catholic Social Thought and the Ignatian Tradition, at the University of San Francisco who kindly invited me to think through these thoughts for the explicit purpose of gathering together this Roundtable. I am also deeply grateful for the hospitable space at the University of San Francisco filled with wonderful students and colleagues who have been deeply interested and engaged in similar shared circles of research. I have been able to think out loud together with my students in my multiple classes over the years, especially my courses in Religion and Environment; Commons: Land, Water and Air; and more recently, Hinduism: Climate. This essay is a draft document of several threads of ideas I am currently working on.

commons? What are the multiple ways in which the issue of climate is related to the commons? How do we parse the problem of the climate, both in understanding it and in responsibly responding to it?[1]

But first, Pope Francis's *Laudato si'* document. It is an astonishing appeal addressed directly to every person on the planet. It is one hundred and eighty-four pages long; it is written in simple, accessible language; it is clear and thorough. When I read it for the first time, I was moved to tears. Here was a global leader who had struck boldly where few had dared to tread, to articulate a highly sophisticated moral call out to caring for our earth home. It brought together economics, ecology, and ethics. There is some hope that this highly charged document may be able to achieve what it is trying to do. Soon after the document was released on May 24, 2015, there have been enthusiastic and supportive responses from Tibetan Buddhists, Jewish rabbis, Islamic mullahs, Hindu organizations, among others.[2] Pope Francis may very well come to be seen as one of the greatest moral thinkers of our present time.

This carefully crafted document reminded me of another Catholic priest I had known for twenty years, from 1982-2002–Ivan Illich.[3] He was an iconoclast, a fiery, controversial intellectual, a social critic, and a historian of ideas, an outspoken critic of our most treasured

---

[1] See Amitav Ghosh, *The Great Derangement: Climate Change and the Unthinkable.* (Chicago: University of Chicago Press, 2016) on the critical lack of imagination in fictional worlds about the climate and Paul Hawken, *Drawdown: The Most Comprehensive Plan Ever Proposed to Reverse Global Warming* (New York: Penguin Books, 2017), one of the most clarifying calls for a collective and deliberate lowering of global carbon output.

[2] See Pope Francis. *Laudato si': On Care of our Common Home* (Vatical City: Librerio Editrice Vaticana, 2015). There are many multi-religious responses to Pope Francis's *Laudato si'*. Here is one excellent sample of an active interreligious dialogue being conducted all around the world: http://irdialogue.org/wp-content/uploads/2016/08/Laudato-Si-Responses-8.14-FINAL.pdf

[3] See these two personal essays on Ivan Illich soon after his death in December 2002, two among many of Ivan Illich's close collaborators (Brown 2003; Nagarajan 2003). See most importantly, David Cayley's two brilliant, ground-breaking books on Ivan Illich (2005, 1992).

certainties. From the early 1950s until he passed away in late 2002, Ivan Illich had firmly and insistently woven together fields of religion, sociology, technology, ethics, equity, ecology, commons and economics, a feat rarely done then or now. He is not as well-known today as he was fifty years ago; nevertheless, I think it is important to bring his ideas more to the fore, as I believe they can be useful and helpful in muddling through our present predicament.

## Ivan Illich and the History of Needs

Ivan Illich (1926-2002) was born in Vienna, Austria to a Catholic father from the Dalmatian Islands in Croatia and a Jewish mother who came from a converted Catholic family, originally from Germany. In the spring of 1984, he related to me the terrors he felt when Nazism arose and took over his worlds in Vienna when he was a teenager from the 1930s to the early 1940s.[4] He described in an anguished voice, decades after it had happened, the force with which he was humiliated in elementary and middle school because of his Jewishness and the terrors of that time. As a teenager, in the early 1940s, during the height of the takeover of Austria by Germany, he helped his family—his mother and his younger twin brothers—escape Vienna, Austria to Florence, Italy. Once he finished high school in Florence, he trained intensively at the Pontifical Gregorian University in Rome in theology and felt the intellectual force of another Catholic priest, Jacques Maritain. Illich subsequently received a Ph.D. in history at the University of Salzburg after WWII. Throughout Illich's life, he actively linked the worlds of the spirit and the material in unique and distinguished ways.

There were three phases to his adult life which were not distinct and separate, but rather, overlapped with each other. From 1951 to 1968, he moved in the world primarily as a Catholic priest. He worked with a Puerto Rican community in Harlem in the 1950s. He became fascinated by the ways in which they had come to

---

4    Personal Conversation, Spring 1984, Pitzer College, Claremont Colleges.

Catholicism with their own unique cultural gifts. He organized one of the biggest Puerto Rican-American Catholic festivals on the Fordham University campus. Subsequently, he became the Vice Rector at the University of Puerto Rico in Puerto Rice. Then, he moved to Cuernavaca, Mexico and started an organization called the Center for Intercultural Formation (CIF) in 1961 which later merged into another organization called CIDOC (Centre for Intercultural Documentation). CIDOC was a Spanish language training center for those in the United States who wanted to learn Spanish. Simultaneously, it was a center that ran seminars and courses on the sustainability of contemporary institutions, the ideas behind western civilization, and the unrecognized strength and vitality in traditional, vernacular cultures. For nearly its entire existence, CIDOC became very famous and attracted students from all over the world. CIDOC lasted until 1976.

Ivan Illich, during this heyday as an activist Catholic priest working for the Church in Mexico, was in an uneasy relationship with the Church at times, as he was outspoken about the western solipsism sometimes embedded within the thinking and acting of the Church when approaching work in the "third world."[5] He did not see the southern countries as "underdeveloped or third world" or as the sole criterion to see people from those lands. He believed in the dignity and spirit of people who had not yet become industrialized, and he constantly advocated a third way for those not yet under the spell of the necessity of the industrial complex.

The second phase of Illich's life involved giving public lectures on what he was thinking about and the writings which emerged from these popular lectures. Illich became a prolific writer during the last decade of CIDOC. His first essay "The Seamy Side of Charity" was published in the Jesuit magazine, *America*, on January 21, 1967. It was one of the earliest essays criticizing the implicit American cultural hegemony at the root of the "desire to help the third world." It is not that Illich advocated to not help those countries outside of the

---

[5]    Ibid.

modern-industrial fold, but rather that we needed to actively recognize that "helping" itself was deeply problematic to begin with, given the different cultural and economic locations of those of us coming from the United States. He believed one needed to be very careful and aware that one's good intentions may very well cause more harm than good and that our own deep, American imperialism may be invisible to ourselves. This essay is now regarded as such a classic that it has become required reading in many different fields.

His subsequent collections of essays included *The Celebration of Awareness: A Call for Institutional Revolution (1970)*, *De-schooling Society* (1970), *Medical Nemesis: The Expropriation of Health, Tools for Conviviality (1973)*, and *Energy and Equity* (1974). These controversial books were sharp, incisive, and devastating critiques of key aspects of industrial civilization, especially in the fields of education, medicine, health, technology, and energy.

He thought in the 1960s and 1970s, like Gandhi, fifty years before, that if everyone in the world consumed at the rate of the western world, it would be not be sustainable. Gandhi had said, in the newspaper he edited, *Young India*, in 1928, "God forbid that India should ever take to industrialism after the manner of the West. If an entire nation of 300 million took to similar economic exploitation, it would strip the world bare like locusts."[6] Instead, Illich advocated for everyone, both in the west and in the south, to rethink the assumptions of the ill thought out industrialized path that seemed nearly messianic in the 1950s and 1960s. He labelled the unquestioned industrialized path as the "idol" moderns worship without thinking. He was not against modernity, as many had misunderstood. He was for a kind of critical modernity, a modernity which we question even as we enter each new unfolding, that we keep everyone in view when we evaluate each new technology and we keep a sharp eye on its invisible assumptions and hegemonies. He was afraid of the implicit "goodness" we believed lay

---

6    Gandhi, Mohandas, Ed. Young India. As quoted in Nandini Joshi, *Development Without Destruction: Economics of the Spinning Wheel* (Ahmedabad, India: Navajivan Publishing House, 1992), 97.

in modernity. He argued again and again that we were proselytizers of a new way of life, without knowing or realizing the rich values and assumptions of other ways of life we were destroying and moreover, how much these other cultural ways could teach us where we were, in fact, blind and deaf.

Next, in his third life phase he began his sharp turn in writing towards history. He moved away from current issues and looked for the sources of our cultural assumptions in historical texts, archives, and other materials. He tried to understand where we had come from, how the very modern assumptions we lived became naturalized into unspoken and hidden (even to ourselves) certainties. For example, in *Towards a History of Needs* (1978), he turned towards understanding the deeper history of our cultural assumptions of actual needs and constructed needs; he traced the conversion of artificially induced desires into culturally necessary needs served by excessive consumption. How did a car become the definition of transportation? He argued consistently for a society organized around the speed of the bicycle, rather than the car. In the phenomenal book, *H20 and the Waters of Forgetfulness* (1985), he presented a history of the sacredness of water in the west, from ancient Roman fountains to the representations of water in paintings in the 19th century. He set out a more nuanced understanding of the history of smells, the toilet, and industrial sewage systems. It brilliantly brings together the history of the toilet and the parallels between the ways in which cities developed their water systems and how we came to understand the fluid runways inside our own bodies. How did sewage and waste get to be seen in the ways that they were?

During the 1980s, Illich became a historian of ideas. I met him in 1982 in Berkeley when he taught a course on gender based on his book of the same name. I did not think his notions of gender were as well thought as they could have been. This book was built on history of feminist thought, but it strangely undercut them, as he bluntly battled feminism and women's increasing power as another aspect of the modern. In this argument, I could not follow him as I, too, was a modern feminist, though I had deep roots in the patriarchal Hindu orthodoxy, which I grew up in. But I could see what he was trying to understand when I thought of the powers of my village grandmother, who held everyone, including my grandfather, in her hand, in the realm of the household. Yet, outside of the threshold of the house, her power fell away nearly completely. He called it "asymmetric complementarity" but his ideas on gender were not well-received. He was trying to link gender with economic theory, what he called the history of the creation of scarcity, of not enough-ness.

Throughout the 1980s, he tried to articulate a unique perception of our industrial civilization from the view of the 12$^{th}$-13$^{th}$ century in Europe. He wanted to know how we got to this point. How did we come to believe the ideas that we, as a culture, hold close to our hearts? He was engaged in unpacking the deep assumptions with which we all live in the world, which we are mostly unaware of. He lectured widely in the 1980s and 1990s. He moved amongst three places: Cuernavaca, Mexico; Penn State University, State College, PA; and Bremen, Germany.

He questioned the central assumptions of the industrialized west. He battled the rigidification of the industrialization of our certainties in these times. He believed that we, as a society, needed to and should exercise much more choice in our selection of what tools we use to satisfy our needs. He believed that we, as a society, should decide what we actually needed, rather than believing in the advertised articulation of our needs or self-serving needs of professionals who wanted us to become dependent on what they were experts of, whether it was education, medicine, technology, or energy. In this phase, he turned to the 12$^{th}$-13$^{th}$ century to give himself a different vantage point to understand contemporary modern society and its underlying assumptions and beliefs. He constantly seemed to ask the vital, important question: How did we get here? If we are here, we can get out of here by thinking and acting together to a different understanding of our actual needs. His training as a Catholic priest, I believe, gave him a strong basis of asceticism, of advocating a radical simplicity of living, of realizing how little one could actually live with and be content. He lived simply, and he advocated a "liberating austerity" in order to live one's life without imposing on the poor. His work emerged out of his theological, historical training, and his genuine curiosity of other cultural understandings of the world. He was critical of entrenched hierarchies and abuses of excessive power wherever he found them.

Unfortunately, for the most part, the world is still under the spell of industrialized lifestyles which uses far more energy than needed and it is possible for all of us to have, given the excessive carbon we have released into the world. It was not that Illich or Gandhi was completely against industrialization or modernity, but rather, they both thought as a society, we needed to slow down and contemplate, to discern, to figure out whether that was the best direction to go. If so, what did we actually need and how were we going to get there in terms of a fairer sense of ecology, equity, and economics that did not leave huge shadows of inaccessibility, poverty and inequality in their wakes? It is deeply related to what Pope Francis articulates so boldly and necessarily in his *Laudato si'*.

In the 1990s, he became focused on the notions of proportionality.[7] Most of us did not understand quite what he meant back then. We would walk away from his erudite lectures on the history of proportionality in music and art and shake our heads, wondering, what did he mean? Now, I think he meant the following: What is the appropriate proportion of the use of energy, technology, institutions for a convivial society? How do we know when we have gone too far in our practices of knowledge, rituals, and culture; how can we recognize as a culture when they become threatening rather than liberating? How do we know when we are using too much carbon and make the necessary adjustments to our actions? How do we recognize

---

7    Illich moved deeply into the history of music, especially the notion of proportionality in music and how that radically changed from the seventeenth century to the eighteenth century. He argued that the music itself became "even tempered." This change paralleled the movement of industrialization of society. We were not all convinced. I found it hard to follow his argument, though there were many who did.

this and move together on containing the damage? It was another way to expand his earlier idea of "thresholds."

He also believed in the power of friendships, the table around which food is served and ideas are shared, in conviviality. In the fall of 1999, I invited him to come to the University of San Francisco as a part of my Davies Forum on the theme, *Voice, Memory and Landscape*. We had over 1000 people at the Presentation Theater (now the Gershwin Theater) and people lined the walls and the steps; they stayed for nearly three hours, listening to him while he swiftly moved amongst his twelve languages and his ideas. He was clearly in pain as he was battling a deadly cancer, and we all sensed it may be the last time we see him. It was to be one of his last public lectures in California. The following year, during fall 2000 and spring 2001, Jerry Brown, when he was Mayor of Oakland, in between his two stints as Governor of California, brought Ivan Illich in a public collaboration he called, *The Oakland Table*.

Ivan Illich died peacefully the next year on December 2, 2002 in Bremen, Germany. He left a legacy of deep insights on our need to lessen our energy use as a way to enhance equity. His advocacy of a "celebration of awareness," of being alert to those who would cunningly make us believe we needed more than we actually needed at a societal level, brought his Catholic priestly values in conversation with secular thinkers for over sixty years.

David Cayley's two brilliant books on Ivan Illich and his ideas do the impossible: They focus on the complex relationships between Illich's social critiques and his theological understandings. In *Ivan Illich: In Conversation*, David Cayley lets his own questions to Illich help unravel Ivan's own insights into his life work. In some ways, it is easier to understand the range of Illich's ideas in this book as it moves in the rhythms of conversations. Cayley, in his second book on Illich, *The Rivers North of the Future*, goes deep into Illich's theological awakenings to help reveal the strong links to his social critiques of aspects of western modernity in its present form. In this book, Illich expounds the Biblical story of the Good Samaritan and reveals the new kind of love that entered with this story of Christ, the

Samaritan who goes beyond his duty to help this stranger on the road and the ambivalent, metaphoric, and civilizational consequences of that beautiful story he loved so much. [8]

\*\*\*

*An embodied narrative of industrial work conditions in fall of 1984*
*From September 1984 to January 1985, I worked various jobs at the Red Star Yeast factory in West Oakland. I moved large, four-foot-high cylindrical bins full of small, brown yeast modules across the factory floor. I slid gigantic, waffle-shaped iron plates dripping with wet yeast streams, which fell furiously into a trapezoid-shaped trough gurgling with fast moving water. I was constantly afraid I would somehow trip and fall into that gushing sound, as we were standing on rickety ladders. Like everyone else, I had a white cap tightly covering my hair so not one strand could escape; thick goggles covering my eyes, a white, chlorinated apron that covered my sweat-filled blue jeans and t-shirt. I moved always in a rush, as if I was constantly running out of time, no matter the task I was doing. Every two hours, we had a fifteen-minute break. This was heavy, physical work, like which I had never done before. It was exhausting and wore me out. I had no energy to think before and after work.*

*A few weeks later, I was assigned to the assembly line at the center of the factory, behind a swiftly moving rubber sheet waist-high. It was a classic factory scene, one that reminded me of films with Charlie Chaplin, or I Love Lucy, where at some point in the story, the assembly line would go too fast and all of whatever they were helping make, whether chocolates or other objects, would fall apart and a mirthful chaos would ensue. Except in this real-live scene, there was no laughter or comedy to relieve the tension. Here, a long, continuous bar of wet yeast packed tight, but still tenderly soft to the touch, almost like soft tofu, would pass by in front of us. The main goal was to take out the badly damaged yeast bars.*

*In the central area of this assembly line work space, there was a two-foot-high set of blades moving swiftly in the shape of a Ferris wheel. The*

---

[8]    See David Cayley, *Ivan Illich in Conversation*, 1992 and *The Rivers North of the Future*, 2005. See also Todd Hartch's *The Prophet of Cuernavaca: Ivan Illich and the Crisis of the West*, 2015).

*long, rectangularly shaped yeast bar would be cut by each swiftly revolving knife, and our job was to put our hands quickly into the rolling knives and clean out the crumbly pieces of yeast that was stuck on the knives. The main reason was so that the machine would not stop. It was always a dangerous task. We were all aware of how sharp our attention had to be, so that we could withdraw our hands a split second before the next sharp knife blade could come down accidentally on our fingers.*

*Once the yeast was cut into one-pound bars, each yeast bar, one after the other, would go by, serenely as if eagerly waiting to be selected and picked by a customer. We were to examine each one for flaws and take the gentle, broken ones out and throw them into waiting containers. Then, the final step was to have the plastic wraps roll around the yeast bars and get glued on.*

*We would then take each of the wrapped yeast bars and pack up one cardboard box after another. After a few weeks of working on this factory line, I noticed that the factory engineer would come by, without looking over at us, and quietly crank up what looked like a wheel on a concrete pillar some distance away. I learned quickly that twice a day, he would speed up the machine. Months rolled by. (One night when I had to go to a very early morning shift, Ivan Illich, who was visiting for a few days, came to drop me off at the factory and during the half hour ride to the factory, he bombarded me with questions about the factory, how it worked, what I did.)*

*One day in early January 1985, despite our cautions, I heard a piercing scream from my fellow worker, also a University of California, Berkeley graduate. She had been a nationally ranked shot-put player and athlete and also worked another job at UPS. She must have been especially tired that day and the machine may have been cranked especially high. I saw from the corner of my eye, that blood sprayed and shot through the yeast near the rolling blades. My fellow worker was holding her hand, screaming with the pain and horror of it all; her fingers had been cut off. We stopped the relentless machine and searched for the bits of her hand through the yeast bits. We found as many pieces as we could. Eventually over the following days and months ahead, they were sewn back together as best as they could be; her right hand would never be the same. It was horrifying, and we* *were all devastated from this terrible accident. How did this happen to our fellow factory worker friend? We were aware that the accident could have happened to any one of us. It just happened to be her that very hour. A few days later, when we could not work on the factory floor because of the trauma involved, I was transferred to a cleaning section. Here, I lost the use of my eyes for a few hours because of a strong acid we were using to clean some products. I left a few days later, realizing that the $10.45/hour I was getting paid was not worth the potential cost of losing a hand or an eye. I stopped working there a few days later.*[9]

I tell this story to illustrate the ideas of "threshold" of Ivan Illich. How do we recognize the thresholds beyond which we should individually and together decide to not cross? When a human life is threatened with disability in the business calculus of a huge corporation, one should be able to say no. Speed as the indicator of success is what Illich objected to. He often called it a key modern addiction. Whether it was time, or space, industrial productivity demanded a certain demand for unquestioning speed. Speed for the sake of speed was the enemy of the good, Illich would argue. It was a factory floor engineer upping the speed of the conveyer belt in order to make more one-pound yeast bars, without considering the health and safety of the workers making those yeast bars. This made me realize this fact in an embodied way. The bottom line did not register the wounds of the factory workers creating the yeast. The human being on the factory line was not a consideration, except as a means to an end; the human being was just a means to earn the profit, not a consideration in their own right.

It was on that concrete floor of the huge Red Star Yeast factory just abutting the West Oakland Bart Station that I encountered with

---

[9]    Interestingly, I began soon after working at the *Friends of the Ganges*, a tiny, grassroots nonprofit, which supported the Swatch Ganga community in Banaras to help clean the river Ganges. This work would become one of the foundations from which my intellectual work would flourish. The questions that emerged from this work led me, years later, to the burgeoning field of Religion and Ecology, of which I have been a part of now for nearly twenty-five years.

my own bodily experience some of these root metaphors of industrial civilization. The rule my body learned to embody during those four months: Speed of production for the sake of speed without any regard to the safety of the human beings who created the industrial product. I was reminded recently of this story with the two Boeing airplane accidents in Ethiopia and Indonesia. The speed of creating the design of this new type of airplane won over the possibility of death of hundreds of passengers from falling airplanes. I think of the increasing number of whale carcasses coming onto our shores; these whales have hundreds of pounds of plastic in their stomachs. They were starving. Somewhere our culture's calculus has failed us. The speed of instant convenience we get every time we use plastic to wrap, to extend the life of food, becomes a killing knife in the stomachs of large and small creatures, creating death wherever it lands, sometime soon after our daily use.

***

"The promotion of environmental and economic justice as interconnected ethical challenges" is one of the six priorities of the International Association of Jesuit Universities (IAJU). According to our thinking and writing prompt, provided by Director Erin Brigham, Michael Garanzini, S.J. states, "By linking the environmental crisis to its roots in economic forces, and calling for an integral environmental humanism, the Church has pointed to *economic, social, political and psychological changes that are necessary if we are to survive in our "common home". (Italics are mine.)*

Illich provided a new kind of language to understand the predicaments we found ourselves in, then and now. He spoke often in his public lectures and his writing of the following ideas: thresholds, liberating austerity, recovery of the commons, and proportionality. The climate problem can be seen as a classic problem of the "tragedy of the commons" variety, espoused by Garrett Hardin. The more cows you put in the pasture, the less grass there is for the cows to eat. And each cowherder, Hardin argued, will keep putting more and more cows until there is no more grass left. The Nobel Prize winning political economist, Elinor Ostrom, argued against such a stark reality. She, as a researcher, discovered that the commons was a much more convivial place, where communities can meet, organize themselves and create their own blueprint for sustainable survival, whether it be fisheries in Central America, irrigation water rights in Asia, etc. So, the central question is how do we create shared local, regional, national, and global governance rules for lowering carbon in the atmosphere?[10] Illich believed that each one of us had an ethical responsibility to "recover the commons" in all its aspects as one strategy to deal with scarcity.

## Thresholds

Illich's threshold concept comes out of the context of the "development" decades following WWII. The word "development" was referred to as a metaphor for a living, growing form and yet, after WWI, it was used as a hierarchically, naturalized construction to elevate modern people as "developed" and the non-modern peoples as "underdeveloped," "primitive," "savage," etc. This was especially done after WWII with Truman's call to help develop the rest of the world, so that they can become more and more similar to the west. The western model was considered the pinnacle of the achievements of human beings. Ivan Illich, along with Wendell Berry, Leopold Kohr, Paolo Friere, and Rachel Carson, questioned these central assumptions of modernity. This is the core critique of Ivan Illich's insights into "needs." He

---

[10]     Elinor Ostrom was one of the leading scholars on the commons. She won a Nobel Prize in economics for her work. See her many books, but especially her key, ground-breaking book, *Governing of the Commons: The Evolution of Institutions for Collective Action*. Cambridge, UK: Cambridge University Press, 1990. See also Vijaya Nagarajan's On the Languages of the Multiple Commons: A Theoretical View. *Worldviews*: 2017. For a clear introduction to the commons from a variety of disciplinary perspectives, see the excellent book: Bollier, David. 2002. *Silent Theft: The Private Plunder of Our Common Wealth*. New York: Routledge and his *The Wealth of the Commons: A World Beyond Market and State*. Amherst, MA: Leveller's Press.

argued in different ways and in different fields, that there is a history of needs, a history of constructed needs and it behooves us to become familiar with its mechanisms so we recognize it when it comes down the road again, which it inevitably will.

In *Energy and Equity*, he states: "It has recently become fashionable to insist on an impending energy crisis. This euphemistic term conceals a contradiction and consecrates an illusion. It masks the contradiction implicit in the joint pursuit of equity and industrial growth. It safeguards the illusion that machine power can indefinitely take the place of bodily power.... To face this contradiction and betray this illusion, it is urgent to clarify the reality the language of crisis obscures: high quanta of energy degrade social relations just as inevitably as they destroy the physical milieu."[11]

He elaborates on the notion of the social threshold in the use of energy:

"The possibility of a third option is barely noticed. While people have begun to accept ecological limits on maximum per capita energy use as a condition for physical survival, they do not yet think about the use of minimum feasible power as the foundation of any of various social orders that would be both modern and desirable. Yet only a ceiling on energy use can lead to social relations that are characterized by high levels of equity. The one option that is presently neglected is the only choice within the reach of all nations.... What is generally overlooked is that equity and energy can grow concurrently *only to a point. Below a threshold* of per capita wattage, motors improve the conditions for social progress. Above this threshold, energy grows at the expense of equity." (my italics)[12]

What is this third option? The "minimum feasible power" that would be both "modern" and desirable" is critical in Illich's worldview. So, though he is falsely accused of being against modernity, he is clearly not.

---

[11]  See Ivan Illich's *Energy and Equity* (Series: Ideas in Progress. London: Calder and Boyars Ltd., 1974, 15) for chapters on "The Energy Crisis," "The Industrialization of Traffic," "Speed-Stunned Imagination," "The Elusive Threshold," among others.

[12]  Ibid, 17.

He is saying that the improvement of tools works to improve peoples' lives "up to a point" and it is up to us in society to figure out how we understand when equity gets overshadowed by increased energy use. He notes that "equity and energy can grow concurrently only to a point. Below a threshold of per capita wattage, motors improve the condition for social progress. Above this threshold, energy grows at the expense of equity."[13] He is making explicit that this knowledge of when this threshold is approached for any tool is important to become aware of as a society. We need to track when each new technology comes into being, and when the tool becomes counterproductive to society. Technology has not had many limits put on its development or creativity. Elsewhere, he speaks of a bicycle speed society. He also saw the bicycle as a metaphor for lots of other technologies. How do we individually and collectively find the "bicycle" edge for our use of technologies?

Illich also speaks of the term "radical monopoly" as referring to "when one industrial production process exercises an exclusive control over the satisfaction of a pressing need, and excludes nonindustrial activities from competition."[14] He explains how a radical monopoly emerges as a way of substituting one type of product for another more traditional use. For example, the car exerts a radical monopoly on traffic, "practically ruling out locomotion on foot or by bicycle in Los Angeles. ... That motor traffic curtails the right to walk...". This car-focused planning emerged as a need for transportation, thereby negating the use of feet or bicycles for moving ourselves around. Feet become lesser than, and because moving feet takes longer to get somewhere, cars monopolize the space that earlier was filled with walkers, making the use of feet obsolete.[15]

In 1983 in a working document, Illich spoke of the disillusionment from the enlightenment goals of yesteryear: "In fact, the ideal of the enlightenment... is now fading. It is fading for two reasons: first

---

[13]   Ibid.
[14]   Ibid, 52.
[15]   Ibid.

because many of us recognize that it has a dark future and second because we understand that its descendance from past ideals is much less legitimate than we assumed." He asks himself:

"How shall I call the opposite project: the reconquest of the right to live in self-limiting communities, that each treasure their own mode of subsistence. Pressed, I would call this project the recovery of the commons. Commons, in custom and law, refer to a kind of space which is fundamentally different from the space of which most ecologists speak. ... The public environment is opposed to the private home. Both are not what the "commons" mean. Commons are a cultural space that lies beyond my threshold and this side of wilderness. Custom defines the different usefulness of commons for each one. The commons are porous. The same spot for different purposes can be used by different people. And above all, custom protects the commons. The commons are not community resources; the commons become a resource only when the lord or community encloses them. Enclosure transmogrifies the common into a resource for extraction, production or circulation of commodities. Commons are as vernacular as vernacular speech. I am not suggesting that it is possible to recreate the old commons. But lacking any better analogy, I speak of the recovery of the commons to indicate how, at least conceptually, [it can be understood]... Truly subsistence-oriented action transcends economic space, it reconstitutes the commons. This is as true for speech that recovers common language as for action which recovers commons from the environment."[16] (Brackets are mine.)

He further argues for a "recovery of the commons" in subtle and explicit ways throughout the rest of his work and his life.

## Gandhi and Illich

Bapu's Hut. It is hard to leave Gandhi out of our picture today. He was another thinker-activist who saw through the consequences of our shared industrial dreams. He learned much from Thoreau. Thoreau,

16   Illich, Ivan. 1983. Eco-Pedagogics and the Commons. April 1, 1983. 9-10. Cuernavaca, Mexico (Unpublished draft of paper for discussion with Jerry Morris in Techno-Politica series).

following Emerson, read many of the earliest English translations of Hindu texts, such as the *Upanishads*, and the *Bhagavad Gita,* becoming one of the Transcendentalists. Thoreau also witnessed the beginnings of the industrial civilization. In some ways, I think of him being at the beginning of the parenthesis of ideas that we are trying desperately to parenthetically close. Strikingly, even as Thoreau was writing *Walden* in his hut near Walden Pond, he heard the whistle of the train going by every afternoon. Laura Walls says in her astounding biography of Thoreau, "In writing Walden, Thoreau encouraged his readers to try the experiment of life for themselves, rather than inheriting its terms from others…Thoreau is often said to have turned to "Nature," but what he actually turned to was, more exactly, the "commons"—spaces that, back then, were still open to everyone: woods, fields, and hilltops, ponds and blueberry thickets, rivers, meadows, trails up nearby mountains, the long open beaches on the Atlantic shore. Nearly all his writings use landforms and watersheds to explore the commons, expanding our shared natural and intellectual heritage until it touches the Cosmos itself."[17]

Gandhi, himself, some decades later, combined Thoreau, Christianity, and the *Bhagavad-Gita* to understand how to wrest India from the British colonialists and created the political tools of satyagraha (truth-force), swaraj (self-rule), ahimsa (nonviolence), among others. Ivan Illich went and stayed briefly in one of Gandhi's ashrams in the 1970s and wrote a beautiful essay, *Bapu's Hut.*[18] Illich was deeply influenced by his Catholic priestly life, and with Gandhi's insights into the failures of western civilization, of excess desires constructed around a wasteful economy, the artificial creation of envy, and the lack of awareness of setting social limits. Illich states, in one of his many travels in India:

---

[17]     See Laura Wall's *Thoreau: A life* (Chicago: University of Chicago Press, 2017, xiii.), for one of the most moving biographies of Thoreau. It is exquisitely written and charts his intellectual and spiritual journey through his writings and activism.

[18]     Illich, Ivan. *Bapu's Hut*; See: https://www.mkgandhi.org/museum/msgofbapuhut.htm

"It is only the people who have some vested interest who refuse to understand it. The rich do not want to understand. When I say rich, I mean all those people who have got conveniences of life which are not available to everybody in common. These are in living, eating and going about. Their modes of consumption are such that they have been deprived of the power to understand the truth. It is to these that Gandhi becomes a difficult proposition to understand and assimilate. They are the ones to whom simplicity does not make any sense. Their circumstances unfortunately do not allow them to see the truth. Their lives have become too complicated to enable them to get out of trap they are in." [19]

He reveals who the "rich" are in this context: They are the ones that use conveniences that are not accessible to all. He adds:

"This hut connotes the pleasures that are possible through being at par with society. Here, self-sufficiency is the keynote. We must understand that unnecessary articles and goods that a man possesses reduce his power to imbibe happiness from the surroundings. Therefore, Gandhi repeatedly said that productivity should be kept within the limits of wants. Today's mode of production is such that it finds no limit and goes on increasing uninhibited. All these we have been tolerating so far but the time has come when man must understand that by depending more and more on machines he is moving towards his own suicide. The civilized world, whether it is China or America has begun to understand that if we want to progress, this is not the way. Man should realize that for the good of the individual as well as of the society, it is best that people keep for themselves only as much as is sufficient for their immediate needs. We have to find a method by which this thinking finds expression in changing the values of today's world. This change cannot be brought about by the pressure of the governments or through centralized institutions. A climate of public opinion has to be created to make people understand that which constitutes the basic society. Today the man with a motor car thinks himself superior to the man with a bicycle though, when we look at it from the point of view of the common norm, it is the bicycle which is the vehicle of the masses. The cycle, therefore, must be given the prime importance and all the planning in roads and transport should

[19]    Ibid.

be done on the basis of the bicycle, whereas the motor car should get a secondary place."[20]

Thoreau, Gandhi, Illich, and Pope Francis articulate with deep clarity what we, as a society, need to do. Reducing our energy desires for the sake of convenience at a collective level, so that the excess production of energy for some is reduced and the not enough energy situation is increased for millions of others on the same planet. We no longer can remain on the path we have been on.

The Green New Deal proposed by the new Congress in February 2019 reflects the moral imperative of Pope Francis's *Encyclical on Climate Change and Inequality* and Ivan Illich's long ago call for a discernment of our energy needs.[21] It is a response to the potentiality of collective death induced by climate change.

---

20  Ibid.
21  https://www.congress.gov/bill/116th-congress/house-resolution/109/text

# Integral Ecology:
# Solidarity Across Differences

SAM MICKEY*

One way to engage the intersection of environmental and economic justice is through an integral approach to ecology, that is, an approach to ecology that includes multiple ways of being and knowing from across academic disciplines, religious and cultural traditions, and everyday life.[1] Pope Francis proposes an integral ecology in his encyclical, *Laudato si': On Care for Our Common Home*, which was released publicly on June 18, 2015. The title of the encyclical is indicative of the scope of integral ecology. "Laudato si'" ("Praise be to you") is a phrase that occurs several times throughout "The Canticle of the Sun" (also known as "Canticle of the Creatures" and "Praises of the Creatures"), which was composed by the Pope's namesake, St. Francis of Assisi. Writing in 1225, St. Francis sings praises to God's

---

* Sam Mickey is an Adjunct Professor of Theology and Religious Studies at the University of San Francisco. He is a consultant for the Forum on Religion and Ecology at Yale, and the Reviews Editor for the journal *Worldviews: Global Religions, Culture, and Ecology*. His work focuses on integrating philosophical, religious, and scientific perspectives on human-Earth relations.

[1] For more on the variety of approaches to integral ecology and the history of that term, see Sam Mickey, Sean Kelly, and Adam Robbert, ed., *The Variety of Integral Ecologies: Nature, Culture, and Knowledge in the Planetary Era* (Albany: SUNY Press, 2017).

creatures as his sisters and brothers, such as Sister Moon, Brother Son, Brother Fire, and Sister Water.[2]

According to the Pope, "Saint Francis is the example par excellence of care for the vulnerable and of an integral ecology lived out joyfully and authentically. [...] Francis helps us to see that an integral ecology calls for openness to categories which transcend the language of mathematics and biology, and take us to the heart of what it is to be human."[3] Integral ecology includes the varieties of scientific perspectives on relations between organisms and environments, and it also involves a sense of kinship like that expressed by St. Francis, a truly cosmopolitan kinship that extends across the differences of all humans and nonhuman creatures in the universe.

For Pope Francis, living out an integral ecology is a matter of faith. It is a spiritual practice of praising creatures, and it coincides with the ethical practice of cultivating equitable and caring relationships with the multifarious denizens of the natural world. "An integral ecology is also made up of simple daily gestures which break with the logic of violence, exploitation and selfishness."[4] Uniting the personal, the social, and the environmental, integral ecology attends to the cries of all those in need, including "*both the cry of the earth and the cry of the poor.*"[5] The Pope is alluding to the Brazilian theologian Leonardo Boff (b. 1938), specifically his work, *Cry of the Earth, Cry of the Poor*, which brings together a wide variety of philosophical, theological, and scientific perspectives that account for the intertwining of environmental and socioeconomic crises. For Boff, theology and ecology converge insofar as they both "seek liberation" in response to cries of suffering from two "bleeding wounds"— social oppression and

---

2    St. Francis of Assisi, "The Canticle of the Sun," in *The Writings of St. Francis of Assisi*, ed. Paschal Robinson (New York: Magisterium Press, 2015), 121.

3    Pope Francis, *Laudato si': On Care for Our Common Home* (Vatican City: Libreria Editrice Vaticana, 2015), 9.

4    Ibid, 166.

5    Ibid, 35.

environmental destruction.[6] Moreover, the term "integral ecology" is itself an allusion to Boff, who used that term approximately twenty years before Pope Francis would release *Laudato si'*. The allusion to Boff is rather obvious, and yet Boff is not mentioned by name, and his work is not cited. This omission is particularly noteworthy, considering that *Laudato si'* is otherwise replete with citations and follows rigorous scholarly standards. Why is the citation to Boff omitted? It is not as if Boff's integral ecology is only a passing idea in the encyclical. Rather, it is the subject of one of the encyclical's six chapters (chapter 4). It is not as if Boff's image of poor and earthly cries is inconsequential for the overall composition of the encyclical. Those cries are mentioned more than once throughout the encyclical, even appearing in the Pope's concluding prayer, "A Christian prayer in union with creation," which ends with the following eight lines:

*The poor and the earth are crying out.*
*O Lord, seize us with your power and light,*
*help us to protect all life,*
*to prepare for a better future,*
*for the coming of your Kingdom*
*of justice, peace, love and beauty.*
*Praise be to you!*
*Amen.*[7]

Boff has been a controversial figure in Catholicism since the early 1980s, when he and other advocates of liberation theology in Brazil were silenced by Cardinal Joseph Ratzinger for their critical views of the far-right government (a military dictatorship supported by the United States) that had held power in Brazil since 1964.[8] The anti-imperial, anti-capitalist, Marxist leanings of liberation theology were seen by Ratzinger as conflicting with Catholic teaching, so much so that mentioning Boff in an encyclical would still be a divisive,

---

6    Leonardo Boff, *Cry of the Earth, Cry of the Poor*, trans. Phillip Berryman (Maryknoll: Orbis Books, 1997), 104.

7    Pope Francis, *Laudato si'*, 160.

8    Jane Kramer, "Daily Comment: What the Pope Can Pray For," *The New Yorker*, February 21, 2013.

controversial act in the twenty-first century. The Pope cannot say Boff's name in the context of an encyclical. To be clear, the Pope does not use the word "capitalism" in the encyclical either, although critiques of "consumerism" abound.

Along with Boff's commitment to anti-capitalist liberation, part of what makes him so controversial is the assemblage of radical thinkers on which he draws to formulate his ideas of liberation theology and integral ecology. This is evident from a consideration of two of his prominent predecessors. One is the cultural historian Thomas Berry (1914-2009), a Catholic priest in the Passionist order who sought a universal vision broader than that provided by Catholicism alone, more inclusive of the wisdom of all religious traditions and more inclusive of the wisdom of the universe itself.[9] Berry was reportedly lecturing about integral ecology and integral cosmology in the early 1990s, before Boff first used the term in print in 1995.[10] The other prominent influence on Boff is Félix Guattari (1930-1992), a French philosopher, psychoanalyst, and political activist who spent time in Brazil in the early 1980s to learn from and support democratic resistance to Brazil's authoritarian government.[11] Guattari's notion of an ecological philosophy ("ecosophy") parallels the framework that Boff envisions for integral ecology, and Guattari is even more emphatically Marxist.

This paper explicates some of what the Pope leaves unsaid, tracing the connections between his integral ecology and the radical visions of Boff, Berry, and Guattari. Outlining these theoretical roots of integral ecology affords a more specific assessment of its potential for

---

[9]  Mary Evelyn Tucker, John Grim and Andrew Angyal, *Thomas Berry: A Biography* (New York: Columbia University Press, 2019).

[10]  Sean Esbjörn-Hargens, "Ecological Interiority: Thomas Berry's Integral Ecology Legacy," in *Thomas Berry, Dreamer of the Earth: The Spiritual Ecology of the Father of Environmentalism*, ed. Ervin Laszlo and Allan Combs (Rochester, VT: Inner Traditions, 2011), 93. On the role of Berry and Boff in Catholic eco-theology, see John Hart, "Catholicism," in *The Oxford Handbook of Religion and Ecology*, ed. Roger Gottlieb (New York: Oxford University Press, 2006), 80–87.

[11]  Félix Guattari and Suely Rolnik, *Molecular Revolution in Brazil*, trans. Karel Clapshow and Brian Holmes (Los Angeles: Semiotext(e), 2007).

addressing the ethical and political challenges posed by interlocking economic and environmental crises across local and global scales. Situating *Laudato si'* within this intellectual lineage opens up multiple possibilities for building alliances across differences. To be sure, whatever is controversial about integral ecology is not antithetical to Catholicism. If anything, it aims to be more catholic, more universal in its address. The Pope's encyclical addresses all Catholics on Earth today, numbering over one billion, and more universally, the Pope is addressing "every person living on this planet."[12]

## On the Way to Integral

The environmental historian Donald Worster (1994) claims that Charles Darwin is the "single most important figure in the history of ecology over the past two or three centuries."[13] Responding to Darwin's evolutionary theory, the German biologist Ernst Haeckel coined the term *oecologie* in 1866, conceiving of this new field as an extension of biological science. The principle of natural selection suggests that species evolve in relationship to environmental conditions. While biology studies organisms, ecology focuses on the relationships between organisms and environments. Ecology can thus be understood as a more complex and comprehensive way to study life, situating life within the "household" (*oikos*) of nature. By focusing on organism-environment interrelations, Haeckel's ecology developed more thorough explanations of the conditions of existence for living beings. Theories and methods of ecology became increasingly thorough in subsequent generations.

The twentieth century saw the emergence of a "new ecology," which included biophysical and socioeconomic sciences to provide "an energy-economic model of the environment," whereby ecologists like Charles Elton and Arthur Tansley used thermodynamics and

---

12    Pope Francis, *Laudato si'*, 4.
13    Donald Worster, *Nature's Economy: A History of Ecological Ideas*, 2nd ed. (New York: Cambridge University Press, 1994), 114.

economic models of efficiency, production, and consumption to describe the flow of energy through an ecological "community" (Elton) or "ecosystem" (Tansley).[14] This approach to ecology was further refined with the inclusion of systems theory and chaos theory into ecology during the 1970s and 1980s. Applied to ecology, those theories showed the important role of disorder and natural disturbances in ecological relationships, such that the energy flows of ecosystems need to be understood not as harmonious or static systems but as changing, unpredictable, unruly, and complex.

In an article first published in *Science* in 1977, Eugene Odum proposed an updated "new ecology," which would be an "integrative discipline," where "integrative" reflects a commitment to complexity and an opposition to oversimplification.[15] Affirming holism and opposing reductionism, "the new ecology links the natural and the social sciences," both in theory and in practice, seeking "to raise thinking and action" to a holistic encounter with ecosystems.[16] Odum follows the energy-economic model of ecology in working toward the "integration of economic and environmental values," but he also goes further, including not only economics but also politics and legal issues within the holistic discipline of integrative ecology.[17] However, Odum's ecology still contains aspects of the reductionism it proclaims to avoid.

Odum envisions an interdisciplinary and engaged ecology, but his vision fails to address the religious or spiritual perspectives on ecology, and it fails to include the humanities. Neglecting those perspectives means neglecting a vast array of experiences, ideas, symbols, artistic expressions, and ways of being in the world. Those perspectives have gradually become more well-represented in environmental theory and practice since the 1970s, specifically with the emergence of philosophical, religious, and literary discourses on the natural world

---

14  Ibid, 311.
15  Eugene Odum, "The Emergence of Ecology as a New Integrative Discipline," in *The Philosophy of Ecology: From Science to Synthesis*, ed. David Keller and Frank Golley (Athens, GA: University of Georgia Press, 2000), 198.
16  Ibid, 199.
17  Ibid, 201.

(e.g., environmental ethics, ecofeminism, deep ecology, ecopoetics, and the field of religion and ecology). Such discourses are collectively known today as the environmental humanities. The promise of integral ecology is to include evermore perspectives, even conflicting and contradictory perspectives.

The phrase "integral ecology" first appeared in published work in 1958, in a marine ecology textbook by Hilary Moore. Moore sought to integrate ecologies that focus on ecosystems (synecology) with ecologies that focus on their component organisms (autecology).[18] Moore's integral ecology gestures toward a common feature of integral approaches to ecology: a commitment to integrate parts and wholes. However, the humanistic, social, and spiritual aspects of ecology are not included in Moore's framework. A more inclusive sense of integral ecology was proposed by Boff along with Virgil Elizondo in a jointly written introduction to an issue of the theology journal *Concilium*, where they say the following:

> The quest today is increasingly for an *integral ecology* that can articulate all these aspects with a view to founding a new alliance between societies and nature, which will result in the conservation of the patrimony of the earth, socio-cosmic wellbeing, and the maintenance of conditions that will allow evolution to continue on the course it has now been following for some fifteen thousand million years.

> For an integral ecology, society and culture also belong to the ecological complex. Ecology is, then, the relationship that all bodies, animate and inanimate, natural and cultural, establish and maintain among themselves and with their surroundings. In this holistic perspective, economic, political, social, military, educational, urban, agricultural and other questions are all subject to ecological consideration. The basic question in ecology is this: to what extent do this or that science, technology, institutional or personal activity, ideology or religion help either to support or to fracture the dynamic equilibrium that exists in in the overall system?[19]

---

[18]   Hilary B. Moore, *Marine Ecology* (New York: Wiley, 1958), 7.
[19]   Leonardo Boff and Virgil Elizondo, "Ecology and Poverty: Cry of the Earth, Cry of the Poor," *Concilium: International Journal of Theology* 5 (1995): ix–x.

Boff has since elaborated on more details of his idea of integral ecology, specifically by situating integral ecology in relationship to three other ecological registers: environmental, social, and mental.[20] The environmental approach engages ecological issues through biophysical sciences and the development of technologies. The social approach includes humans and society within ecological issues, addressing problems of social justice and cultivating sustainable social institutions (education, healthcare, economic development, etc.). The mental approach focuses on subjectivity, showing how ecological problems call not only for a healthier and more sustainable society and environment, but also for healthier ways of thinking, feeling, and acting. Like ecopsychology and deep ecology, what Boff calls mental ecology speaks to the soul, whereas the previous two ecologies speak to the soil and society.

Those three ecologies (environmental, social, and mental) represent the multiple perspectives that have emerged from the biophysical sciences, social sciences, and humanities, respectively. The integral approach brings together those multiple ecologies to present a new vision of planetary coexistence. It is a vision of humans and Earth emerging from the evolutionary becoming of the universe, which is to say, processes of cosmogenesis, which include three aspects: (a) complexity and differentiation, which structures the objective or exterior facets of things; (b) self-organization and consciousness, which structures the subjective depth or interior facets of things; and (c) reconnection and relation, which structures the ways things come together not merely as a collection of different objects but as communing agents, communicating subjects. Those three aspects of cosmogenesis correlate with the soil, soul, and society of the three ecologies. They also indicate Boff's indebtedness to his predecessors, as the next sections make clear.

---

20    Leonardo Boff, "Interview: Leonardo Boff, a Founder of Liberation Theology," *Kosmos Journal*, September 6, 2016.

# Integral Ecologist as Spiritual Guide

Boff's idea of three aspects of cosmogenesis draws upon the integral vision developed by Berry, who similarly articulates "three basic principles: differentiation, subjectivity, and communion."[21] Those principles are presented as the "cosmogenetic principle" in Berry's work with the cosmologist Brian Swimme, *The Universe Story*.[22] In terms of the cosmogenetic principle, all evolutionary processes in the universe involve an objective side, that is, an exterior that differentiates things from one another, as well as a subjective side. The subjective side includes the activities of self-organization that constitute the interiority or agency of things, and the relational interactions whereby all subjects in the universe exist in community or communion. Differentiation can be seen in the diversity of life and the uniqueness of every single being. The subjective dimension of things can be understood in terms of scientific conceptions of self-organization (autopoiesis) as well as in terms of religious traditions that articulate the ensouled or numinous element of reality. An experience of this numinous quality is crucial for Berry's integral vision: "What is important is the attainment of a conscious realization of the spiritual nature of human development. Only then can a truly integral human experience be achieved."[23]

For the most part, Berry's explicit use of the phrase "integral ecology" seems to have occurred in lectures and conversations, not published texts. One exception to this is his 1996 essay on "An Ecologically Sensitive Spirituality," which was published in his book, *The Sacred Universe*.[24] In that essay, Berry proposes that the integral ecologist is a guide for our current historical moment. The

---

21    Thomas Berry, *The Great Work: Our Way into the Future* (New York: Bell Tower, 1999), 162.

22    Brian Swimme and Thomas Berry, *The Universe Story: From the Primordial Flaring Forth to the Ecozoic Era—A Celebration of the Unfolding of the Cosmos* (San Francisco: HarperCollins, 1992), 66-78.

23    Thomas Berry, *The Sacred Universe: Earth, Spirituality, and Religion in the Twenty-First Century*, ed. Mary Evelyn Tucker (New York: Columbia University Press, 2009), 15.

24    Ibid, 129-138.

integral ecologist guides our awakening to the profound complexity and numinous mystery of the Earth community. Along these lines, Berry proposes "an ecological spirituality with an integral ecologist as spiritual guide."[25]

> The integral ecologist can now be considered a normative guide for our times. The integral ecologist would understand the numinous aspect of a universe emergent from the beginning. [...] The integral ecologist is the spokesperson for the planet in both its numinous and its physical meaning, just as the prophet was the spokesperson for the deity, the yogi for the interior spirit, and saint for the Christian faith. In the integral ecologist, our scientific understanding of the universe becomes a wisdom tradition.[26]

Bringing together wisdom, experience, and know-how, the integral ecologist communicates narratives whereby we humans might "accept that we exist as an integral member of this larger community of existence".[27] Moreover, the spirituality of this endeavor is by no means otherworldly: "Religion takes its origin here in the deep mystery of what we see, hear, touch, taste, and savor."[28] The numinous quality of the universe is a mystery not because it is far away or transcendent, but because it is so close, so intimate that it remains ungraspable.

When Berry defines the integral ecologist as a spiritual guide for our times, he says that the "great spiritual mission of the present is to renew all the traditional religious-spiritual traditions in the context of the integral functioning of the biosystems of the planet."[29] Berry then goes on to say that an example of the realization of this mission can be seen in a project that began in the 1990s at the Center for the Study of World Religions (CSWR) at Harvard and that led to the formation of the Forum on Religion and Ecology (FORE), which is currently stationed at Yale.

---

[25]   Ibid, 135.
[26]   Ibid, 136.
[27]   Ibid, 138.
[28]   Ibid, 147.
[29]   Ibid, 136.

The Forum is comprised of a diverse network of scholars, researchers, activists, advocates, and religious practitioners. Since its beginnings, the Forum's work has engaged the multiple religious traditions of the world, an engagement that is represented in the book series on Religion of the World and Ecology based on a series of conferences between 1996 and 1998 and published through the CSWR at Harvard. The series explored ecological implications of Christianity, Judaism, Islam, Hinduism, Buddhism, Jainism, Confucianism, Daoism, Shinto, and indigenous traditions, and with that comprehensive effort, the series contributed to the development of "a new field of study in religion and ecology."[30] The Forum website developed around the conference and book series "to assist in fostering research, education, and outreach in the area of religion and ecology."[31]

Committed to crossing between and beyond disciplinary boundaries, the Forum engages with a wide array of ecologically oriented academic fields related not only to religious studies and the humanities but also to social and natural sciences. The founders and coordinators of the Forum are Mary Evelyn Tucker and John Grim. In their account of the conceptual and organizational beginnings of the Forum and of the field of religion and ecology, Berry's life and work play a crucial role. Tucker and Grim both studied with Berry while he was directing the Fordham University graduate program (MA and PhD) in History of Religions and "the Riverdale Center of Religious Research along the Hudson river just north of New York City," where they would all meet "for meals and conversation."[32] Berry oriented his students, Tucker and Grim among them, to the work of "exploring the cosmology of religions, namely the ways in which the power and

---

30    Mary Evelyn Tucker, "Religion and Ecology: Survey of the Field," in *The Oxford Handbook of Religion and Ecology*, ed. Roger Gottlieb (Oxford: Oxford University Press, 2007), 407.

31    Ibid, 410.

32    John Grim and Mary Evelyn Tucker, "Intellectual and Organizational Foundations of Religion and Ecology," in *Grounding Religion: A Field Guide to the Study of Religion and Ecology*, ed. Whitney Bauman, Richard Bohannon, and Kevin O'Brien (New York: Routledge, 2011), 82.

beauty of the surrounding universe evoked in peoples a response in story, symbol, and ritual."[33]

The integrative perspective on cosmology and religion that Berry conveyed to Tucker and Grim is something that Berry appreciated in the work of Pierre Teilhard de Chardin (1881-1955), a French Jesuit paleontologist whose theology made controversial and groundbreaking contributions to the integration of the Christian faith with scientific understandings of evolution. Grim and Tucker write, "For Teilhard the universe is the 'divine milieu' at one with the evolutionary process."[34] Citing Teilhard numerous times throughout *Cry of the Earth, Cry of the Poor*, Boff finds Teilhard's evolutionary spirituality useful for the project of integral liberation. More generally, Teilhard's panentheistic integration of science and spirituality continues to have a growing influence in the twenty-first century.[35]

Pope Francis cites Teilhard in *Laudato si'*, as Teilhard would support the Pope's comment that "the fullness of God" is the "ultimate destiny of the universe," a destiny that "has already been attained by the risen Christ."[36] It is worth noting that the name Teilhard is mentioned only in a footnote, which seems appropriate considering that Teilhard's work was considered highly controversial by the Catholic Church throughout the twentieth century, particularly because of his panentheistic vision for which God and nature are intimately intertwined, coming dangerously close to the heretical idea of pantheism, which collapses the distinction between God and nature. Controversial Catholics like Boff, Berry, and Teilhard open up tremendous potentials for integrating religion and science and for developing comprehensive responses to the intersecting environmental, economic, and existential crises of this current evolutionary moment. The fact that the Pope can refer to them only obliquely is a testament to their potential for radical transformation.

---

33   Ibid.
34   Ibid, 83.
35   Arthur Fabel and Donald St. John, ed. *Teilhard in the 21st Century: The Emerging Spirit of Earth* (Maryknoll: Orbis Books, 2005).
36   Pope Francis, *Laudato si'*, 58.

# Solidarity

Along with the lineage of Berry and Teilhard, Boff also draws on another lineage of radical thought, that of the French philosopher Félix Guattari. Well before he traveled to Brazil during the revolutionary activity of the early 1980s, Guattari was already heavily involved in political activism. He was very active with protests and demonstrations during the May 1968 events in France, which were oriented around anti-capitalist and anti-consumerist sentiments. Guattari co-wrote several books with the philosopher Gilles Deleuze (1925-1995), including a two-volume book of anti-capitalist theory (*Capitalism and Schizophrenia*). Guattari reconfigures Marxist thought and practice for an era of globalization, multiculturalism, communication and information technologies, and environmental degradation.[37] With Guattari, integral ecology is the antidote to the psychospiritual, economic, and environmental catastrophes of global capitalism.

In *The Three Ecologies* (initially published in French in 1989, *Trois Écologies*), Guattari proposes a "generalized ecology" or "ecosophy" that would seek to reinvent human practices in their relationship to material conditions, social relationships, and subjectivity.[38] Just like Boff's environmental, social, and mental ecologies parallel Berry's cosmogenetic principle, they also parallel Guattari's three ecologies. Boff is explicit on this point. The violent actions of humans toward the natural world indicate "a failure to integrate the three main directions of ecology as formulated by F. Guattari: environmental ecology, social ecology, and mental ecology."[39] Integrating the three ecologies

---

[37] For a detailed account of the ecological implications of the writings of Deleuze and Guattari in comparison with Berry, see Sam Mickey, *Whole Earth Thinking and Planetary Coexistence: Ecological Wisdom at the Intersection of Religion, Ecology, and Philosophy* (New York: Routledge, 2015).

[38] Félix Guattari, *The Three Ecologies*, trans. Ian Pindar and Paul Sutton (London: Ahtlone Press, 2000), 28-37, 52.

[39] Boff, *Cry of the Earth, Cry of the Poor*, 216.

requires what Guattari calls "transversal tools"—experimental practices whereby individuals and communities can cross boundaries to achieve communication between multiple levels or registers of meaning.[40] For Boff, transversality is the "feature of ecological knowledge" that moves across multiple domains of knowledge at the same time, relating "laterally (ecological community), frontward (future), backward (past), and inwardly (complexity) all experiences and all forms of comprehension."[41]

Guattari also develops his concept of ecosophy in his final book, *Chaosmosis*, which poses a fundamental question to guide ecosophy:

> how do we change mentalities, how do we reinvent social practices that would give back to humanity—if it ever had it—a sense of responsibility for its own survival, but equally for the future of all life on the planet, for animal and vegetable species, likewise for incorporeal species such as music, the arts, cinema, the relation with time, love and compassion for others, the feeling of fusion at the heart of the cosmos?[42]

Guattari's mental ecology not only includes ideas and cognition, but the full spectrum of cognitive and affective processes whereby subjectivity articulates itself and participates in embodied engagements with the world and with "the 'mysteries' of life and death."[43] Guattari proposes that mental ecology focus on "the promotion of innovatory practices" and "alternative experiences," which respect the unique singularity of subjects and create appropriate relations between subjects and society.[44]

Social ecology addresses the collective processes of subjectivity, what Guattari calls processes of "singularization" and "subjectification."[45]

---

[40]   Guattari, *The Three Ecologies*, 69.
[41]   Boff, *Cry of the Earth, Cry of the Poor*, 4.
[42]   Félix Guattari, *Chaosmosis: An Ethico-Aesthetic Paradigm*, trans. Paul Bains and Julian Pefanis (Bloomington: Indiana University Press, 1995), 119-120.
[43]   Guattari, *The Three Ecologies*, 35.
[44]   Ibid, 59.
[45]   Ibid, 45.

Addressing events such as "sudden mass consciousness-raising," transformative social struggles, technology, media, and labor, social ecology promotes creative subjectivity that overcomes exploitative and oppressive powers.[46] Between mental and social ecology, the question of ecosophy becomes one of "the whole future of fundamental research and artistic production," a question of "how to encourage the organization of individual and collective ventures" that care for the singularity of subjectivity.[47] Guattari's environmental ecology attends to the complexities and uncertainties of environmental processes, affirming that "anything is possible—the worst disasters or the most flexible evolutions."[48] Drawing on systems sciences, Guattari attends to the complexity and openness of self-organizing (autopoietic) systems as affective assemblages, which have interrelated parts and enable different ways of acting and being acted upon. He thus avoids any reduction of human or nonhuman beings to mere objects.

The scope of the three ecologies embraces all assemblages and the complex relations in and between them, spanning the human and the nonhuman, across all scales of existence. This supports the creation of new ethical and political practices that integrate humans and nonhumans into resilient forms of solidarity.[49] Integrating "the tangled paths of the tri-ecological vision," Guattari's ecosophy aims for creative transformations in both the collective unity and singular differences between individuals (including human and nonhuman individuals), such that ecosophy aims for all individuals to "become both more united and increasingly different" (pp. 67–69). Putting the cosmos back in cosmopolitanism, ecosophy welcomes humans to undertake collective experiments in intellectual, emotional, and physical intimacy with the universe.

When Pope Francis calls for "ecological conversion" in *Laudato si'*, he is not simply enjoining people to study scientific perspectives on society and the environment, and he is not only instructing Catholics

---

46    Ibid, 62.
47    Ibid, 65.
48    Ibid, 66.
49    Ibid, 66-67.

to be more attentive to environmental issues like global warming.[50] More than that, he is calling for the worldwide emergence of ecological forms of consciousness and culture. He is calling for humans to *be* ecological, to live out authentically and joyfully the kinship that all members of humankind have with one another and with all other kinds of creatures. This is something that humans have never done, at least not on a planetary scale. People like Boff, Berry, and Guattari make this clear: integral ecology is the most immense challenge that the human species has ever faced. This involves a reorientation of civilization away from the desires for human dominance and for otherworldly transcendence, desires that have held sway throughout much of the historical period of human evolution. Integral ecology calls for the multiplication of new desires, grounded in intimate relationships with the life, land, air, and water of Earth, and open to the stars, planets, and indeed, the whole universe.

In conclusion, consider a few of the radical implications of integral ecology. More than a recognition of interconnections between environmental and economic systems, integral ecology is a practice of universal solidarity. It is a call for the development of an ecological sense of self, a spiritual relationship with the evolving cosmos, and a political revolution that facilitates anti-capitalist liberation for all members of the Earth community.

---

[50]     Pope Francis, *Laudato si'*, 140.

# 'Degrowing' Agriculture: Engaging the Global South with a Growing Northern Social Movement

ADRIENNE JOHNSON* AND BRIAN DOWD-URIBE**

*'Indeed, degrowth in the North will liberate ecological space for growth in the South. Poverty in the South is the outcome of the exploitation of its natural and human resources at low cost by the North. Degrowth in the North will reduce the demand for, and the prices of, natural resources and industrial goods, making them more accessible to the developing South. However, degrowth should be pursued in the North, not in order to allow the South to follow the same path, but first and foremost in order to*

---

*    Adrienne Johnson is an Assistant Professor of Environmental Studies at the University of San Francisco. She specializes in critical approaches to environmental governance in both Ecuador and Indonesia, and teaches courses on nature-society relations and environmental justice. She has published in *Geoforum, Development and Change, Journal of Rural Studies,* and *Latin American Geography.* She is co-editor of a special issue of *Environment and Planning E* on post/anti-colonial and feminist reflections on the methods and methodologies of natural resource industries fieldwork.

**    Brian Dowd-Uribe is an Associate Professor and Academic Director of the MA in International Studies program at the University of San Francisco. His current research explores the social, agro-ecological and economic dimensions of food, agriculture and water policy, primarily in sub-Saharan Africa and Central America.

*liberate conceptual space for countries there to find their own trajectories to what they define as the good life.'* [1]

## 1. Introduction

Global social and ecological crisis has triggered the search for alternatives to the current world order. Mass extinction, rapid biodiversity loss, extreme temperature variability, and rising sea levels are just a few examples of environmental catastrophes that many argue are driven by the excesses of a capitalist world system. Recently, activists and scholars have forwarded a post-capitalist set of principles under the banner of 'degrowth' to address this crisis. In brief, degrowth refers to a predominately Global North social movement that advocates for higher quality of life, rather than GDP growth and material consumption, as the appropriate organizing goal for a just and sustainable society.[2] The degrowth movement positions itself as a counterpoint to ecomodernism, a philosophy which advocates for the quick adoption of green technologies and decoupled economic growth as the way to address our ecological ills.[3] By contrast, degrowth advocates a push for wealth redistribution and a radically smaller resource and energy throughput in a remade society organized according to principles of small-scale production and localization. The influence of the degrowth movement, particularly in European left wing politics, is a subject of growing global attention.[4]

---

[1] G. D'alisa, F. Damaria, G. Kallis, Eds., *Degrowth: A Vocabulary for a New Era* (New York; London: Routledge, 2015), 5.

[2] G. Kallis, V. Kostakis, S. Lange, B. Muraca, S. Paulson, & M. Schmelzer, "Research On Degrowth" in *Annual Review of Environment and Resources*, 43:1 (2018): 291-316.

[3] John Asafu-Adjaye et al., "An ecomodernist manifesto," April 2015, http://www.ecomodernism.org/

[4] John Cassidy, "Can We Have Prosperity Without Growth?" February 3, 2020, https://www.newyorker.com/magazine/2020/02/10/can-we-have-prosperity-without-growth

As the degrowth movement expands, much scholarly attention has been focused on the application of degrowth principles to areas such as economics, technology, and democracy, with an emphasis on the Global North. While discussions on degrowth transitions in these realms are important, we argue that the topic of agriculture, and in particular agriculture in the Global South, is a significant topic that has yet to be discussed in a robust way.[5] Moreover, whether and how the degrowth movement engages the Global South and Southern movements is receiving increased critical scrutiny.[6] In the spirit of informing how the degrowth movement might think through engagements with the South, we ask, 1) **What are the ways in which the Global North and South are linked in relation to agriculture? 2) How might the degrowth movement be shaped via an active and explicit engagement with Northern and Southern linkages in agriculture?**

We begin to tentatively answer these questions through an examination of agriculture in Costa Rica and Ecuador, drawing from our significant engagement with agriculture in both countries. Each nation is celebrated by Northern degrowth activists as a representation of what is possible with dramatically lower levels of capital throughput in the economy. Costa Rica is championed for its social welfare state with high health outcomes and levels of happiness. Similarly, Ecuador is celebrated for its alternative "end goal" for economic development rooted in the concept of *buen vivir*. We contend that a continued engagement with these cases, and specifically their agricultural spaces and histories, may assist in shaping the degrowth project in a way that is more attentive to the ecologies, power relations, and political dynamics of the Global South. Specifically our analysis proposes

---

[5]   With important exceptions, notably Gerber (2020).

[6]   A. Escobar, "Degrowth, postdevelopment, and transitions: a preliminary conversation" in *Sustainability Science*, 10:3 (2015): 451-462. P. Nirmal & D. Rocheleau, "Decolonizing degrowth in the post-development convergence: Questions, experiences, and proposals from two Indigenous territories" in *Environment and Planning E: Nature and Space*, 2:3 (2019), 465-492.

two themes for further consideration and elaboration: histories and markets. These are developed below first through two short agricultural vignettes of each country and in a synthesis section which follows.

## 2. Cases - Costa Rica and Ecuador

### 2.1. Costa Rica

One way of understanding the transformation of agriculture and agricultural spaces in Costa Rica is to examine in closer detail Costa Rica's most common food dish - the *casado*. This dish, customarily eaten at lunch time, consists of a protein, commonly chicken, beef or pork, coupled with rice, beans, fried plantain, a tortilla and a revolving number of side dishes. Though the ingredients for this dish have historically come from Costa Rican farms, they increasingly come from elsewhere - a product of the neoliberalization of Costa Rican agriculture. The small and localized farm systems championed by degrowth advocates can learn from the processes transforming them in a place like Costa Rica, and the role the Global North has played and continues to play in these transformations.

After Costa Rica's 1948 democratic revolution, the central government enacted state policies that were both emblematic of appropriate economic policies at the time, and which celebrated the small farmer as the backbone of Costa Rican democracy. In the coffee sector, these took the form of heavy taxes on "coffee barons" - those who controlled the processing of raw coffee beans; the funds derived from these taxes have famously been linked to investments in health and education that continue to produce comparatively high literacy rates and life expectancy. Wide-ranging state regulation of agriculture also extended to staple crops such as maize and beans, which were purchased from small farmers at inflated prices, and then resold in government-operated dispensaries at subsidized prices for urban consumers. This system allowed small-scale farmers to sustain and even extend their economic footing. For example, the proportion of small farmers as a total percentage of total coffee producers grew from 32-53% from 1960-1973.[7]

But many of these policies came to an end with the enactment of two structural adjustment program (SAP) loans in the 1980s. Countries throughout the Global South struggled with rising inflation and fuel prices, at a time of heavy government spending, and Costa Rica is a quintessential and early example. To avoid defaulting and pay its debtors, Costa Rica negotiated its first SAP loan in 1982 - which endeavored to reduce domestic spending, with agriculture as a main target. The second SAP loan enacted in 1986 ushered in a new agricultural policy titled "Agriculture for Change" - which shifted agricultural incentives towards export growth. Price controls for food staples and their subsidized sale via government-run dispensaries ended along with preferential loans for small-scale production. New incentives were provided for export-oriented crops, such as palm oil, high-value vegetables, and, most recently, pineapple. Pineapple - a crop that was seldom grown as late as the 1990s, has become an $800 million industry; Costa Rica is now the number one exporter of pineapple in the world.[8]

Accompanying these domestic transformations was a simultaneous reduction in tariffs for agricultural imports, further transforming agricultural production. The United States Agency for International Development began providing food aid in the 1980s - in part to secure Costa Rica as a beacon of democracy while attempting to oust the Sandinista government in neighboring Nicaragua. This aid transitioned to the sale of US agricultural products - principally maize, but also beans, putting Costa Rican and US maize and bean producers in direct competition. Since 1961 maize production in

---

[7]   N. Babin, "Agrarian Questions, Neoliberalism and the Persistence of the Costa Rican Coffee Peasantry" in Fletcher, Dowd-Uribe, and Aistara (eds) *Lessons from the Eco-Laboratory* (University of Arizona Press, 2020).

[8]   R. Galt, "The Costa Rican Agrifood System, 1961-2014: Assessing Neoliberalism's Impacts on Agriculture and Diets" in Fletcher, Dowd-Uribe, and Aistara (eds) *Lessons from the Eco-Laboratory* (University of Arizona Press, 2020).

Costa Rica has fallen 86% and bean production 54%.[9] There is now a common pair of gringos on the plate of the Costa Rican *casado* - the tortilla and the beans.

The protein on the Costa Rican casado has also been a locus of change from these processes. The chicken sector has changed dramatically over the last several decades with flock size of chicken farms growing 14-fold from 1963 to 2014 in 2013.[10] Now, almost 30% of all Costa Rican chickens come from US-style Confined Animal Feeding Operations.[11] Pork has also seen dramatic, and more recent changes. Due to the Central American Free Trade Agreement, the deep fried pork central to one of Costa Rica's famous regional dishes - *chifrijol* - increasingly is imported from the United States. US pork producers are in direct competition from the pork producers in the Puriscal region, where the dish originated.

These processes have left few options for the former producers of the Costa Rican *casado*. It is important to note that these transformations were not passively accepted, but rather, were the central subject of political battles and protest.[12] The movements organized around resistance to the changes, and the political saliency of small-scale agriculture allowed for some programs to survive the rapid neoliberalization of agricultural policy. One such program - the heavily government regulated federal farmers market program - provides one of the major remaining outlets for small farmers to maintain a viable agriculturally-based livelihood.[13] Over 8,000 small farming households sell produce in Costa Rica's farmers market program - the most popular place for Costa Ricans to purchase their

---

[9]   Babin, "Agrarian Questions."

[10]  Galt, "The Costa Rican Agrifood System."

[11]  Ibid.

[12]  M. Edleman, *Peasants Against Globalization: Rural Social Movements in Costa Rica* (Palo Alto: Stanford University Press, 1999).

[13]  B. Dowd-Uribe, & E. Raser, "Costa Rica's Farmers' Market Program: Aiding farmer Livelihoods and Urban Food Security?" in Fletcher, Dowd-Uribe, and Aistara (eds) *Lessons from the Eco-Laboratory* (University of Arizona Press, 2020).

produce (PIMA 2016). Moreover, organic small farmers successfully mobilized for a national organic standard - another lifeline for small farmers who increasingly have few options to continue in agriculturally-based livelihoods.[14]

## 2.2. Ecuador

Discussions on agriculture in Ecuador would not be complete without examining the contours of class, market relations and political organization as related to historical patterns of agricultural development and extraction in Ecuador.[15] These entanglements provide important context surrounding the country's current dedication to the expansion of the palm oil industry. The country's natural resource sector has been marked by three major cycles involving cacao, bananas, and oil, respectively. Between 1860 and 1920, cacao was grown in large quantities along the coastal regions of the country on estates owned by landlord elites who relied on the availability of cheap labor. By the 1920s and 1930s, cacao prices dropped leading to a bust and eventually major bankruptcies. From 1948 until 1965, Ecuador's agricultural sector was dominated by exceptionally large and foreign-owned enterprises linked to the rise of the country's banana boom.[16] By the 1970s and 1980s, a series of technological changes had reduced the size of the banana sector workforce by almost a third in 1983

---

[14]   G. Aistara, "Seeding Organic Sovereignties in the Face of Free Trade" in Fletcher, Dowd-Uribe, and Aistara (eds) *Lessons from the Eco-Laboratory* (University of Arizona Press, 2020).

[15]   M.A. Albán, & H. Cárdenas, *Biofuels Trade and Sustainable Development: The Case of Ecuador's Palm Oil Biodiesel*, Working Paper (International Institute for Environment and Development, 2007) and Francisco Figueroa de la. Vega "'Tablero de comando' para la promocion de los biocombustibles en Ecuador" (*CEPAL*, 2008).

[16]   C. Larrea, & L. North, "Ecuador: Adjustment Policy Impacts on Truncated Development and Democratisation" in *Third World Quarterly*, 18:5 (1997): 913-934 and S. Striffler, *In the Shadows of State and Capital: The United Fruit Company, Popular Struggle, and Agrarian Restructuring in Ecuador, 1900-1995* (Durham; London: Duke University Press, 2002).

and cut the wages of remaining workers. The petroleum boom of the 1970s and 1980s had a significant impact on Ecuador's economic base, shifting governmental investment goals towards those related to large-scale manufacturing and industrial sectors.

Financial gains from the sale of oil enabled the government to invest in welfare programs, infrastructure, and communications through import substitution industrialization programs. In rural spaces, oil revenue helped secure loans for the implementation of a national development approach known as integrated rural development (or DRI – *el Programa de Desarollo Rural Integrado*) which aimed to alleviate poverty by strengthening economic infrastructure and increasing agricultural activity through technical and social means.[17] In the late 1980s and early 1990s though, the falling global prices of crude, debt crisis, and the disappointing and uneven results of DRI projects which resulted in the declining rates of peasant agricultural production prompted the national government to intensify domestic oil production. Pressure from international lending institutions to deregulate the oil industry in combination with a lack of financial resources pushed the government to seek out foreign capital to boost oil flows and to set Ecuador on the path to neoliberalization.[18] The oil industry continues to be a driving force behind the encroachment of indigenous territory by oil companies, which has led to massive deforestation and the contamination of water sources due to drilling activities.[19]

The election of Rafael Correa as Ecuador's new president in 2007 signaled new promise for a reshaping of the country's political future as he was democratically elected on the basis of his bold 'anti-

---

[17] A. Bebbington, & T. Perreault, "Social Capital, Development, and Access to Resources in Highland Ecuador" in *Economic Geography*, 75:4 (1999): 395-418.

[18] S. Sawyer, *Crude Chronicles: Indigenous Politics, Multinational Oil, And Neoliberalism in Ecuador* (Durham and London: Duke University Press, 2004).

[19] M. Bozigar, C. L. Gray, & R. E. Bilsborrow, "Oil extraction and indigenous livelihoods in the Northern Ecuadorian Amazon" in *World development*, 78 (2016), 125-135.

neoliberal' political platform. Along with other left-leaning South American presidents at the time, Correa enacted several political reforms that capture a combination of Keynesian welfare politics, socialism and social democracy in what is often referred to as the 'post-neoliberalism' project.[20] Drawing from the concept of *Buen Vivir* - a concept which is rooted in the Andean cosomovision meaning "plentiful life" or "good living"[21] - Correa enshrined innovative rights in the constitution that would guarantee things such as universal health care and education, food and energy sovereignty, a healthy environment, participation, as well as the right to water and housing.[22] Despite, however, the transformative claims and objectives of Correa's re-founding of Ecuador, many questioned the logics underlying such changes. To some, the newness of a post-neoliberal framework remained questionable[23] as economic policies involving the extractive and agricultural industries did not signal a dramatic shift towards a new economic model but rather repeat many of the same historical dependencies on authoritarian resource extraction.

Many argue that Correa's presidency and the election of Ecuador's newest leader (Lenín Moreno in 2017) has simply reinscribed the country's dedication to resource extraction (both agricultural and oil-

[20]   J. Grugel, & P. Riggirozzi, (2012), "Post-neoliberalism in Latin America: Rebuilding and Reclaiming the State after Crisis" in *Development and Change*, 43:1 (2012): 1-21 and A.M.Y. Kennemore and G. Weeks, "Twenty-First Century Socialism? The Elusive Search for a Post-Neoliberal Development Model in Bolivia and Ecuador" in *Bulletin of Latin American Research*, 30:3 (2011): 267-281.

[21]   Escobar, "Degrowth, postdevelopment, and transitions: a preliminary conversation."

[22]   M. Friant, & J. Langmore, "The Buen Vivir: A Policy to Survive the Anthropocene?" in *Global Policy*, 6:1 (2015): 64-71.

[23]   D.H. Bebbington, & A.J. Bebbington, "Extraction, Territory, and Inequalities: Gas in the Bolivian Chaco" in *Canadian Journal of Development Studies*, 30:1-2 (2010): 259-280, Kennemore and Weeks, "Twenty-First Century Socialism?, R. Burbach, "Ecuador's Popular Revolt: Forging a New Nation" in NACLA Report on the Americas 40 (2007): 4-9 and C. Walsh, C. "Development as Buen Vivir: Institutional Arrangements and (De)colonial Entanglements" in *Development*, 53 (2010): 15–21.

based) as evidenced by the expansion of oil extraction activities in the biodiversity-rich national park of Yasuní but also by the bolstering of 'alternative energy' sectors as related to 'green fuels' such as palm oil. In both industries, the integration of buen vivir principles into the economy has led to, on the one hand, an increase in social services, but on the other hand, a lack of redistribution of the means of production.[24] In recent years, Ecuador has become Latin America's second largest producer of palm oil, in part, due to governmental objectives to shift to a 'post-oil' economy along with growing demand from Europe however the intensification and extensification of plantations has caused much socio-environmental damage.[25] Activists, communities, and scholars continue to resist the contamination of water systems, destruction of forests, and legal and illegal "land-grabbing" practices as linked to the palm oil industry.

## 3. Agriculture: Exploring Northern-Southern Linkages

Below we identify two under-examined themes in degrowth literature related to agriculture in the Global South. Specifically, these themes reflect ways in which the Global South and North are linked, which will have implications for how a degrowth project related to agriculture is envisioned. We point to areas where more analysis should be directed in order for the degrowth project to speak to, and connect with, the realities of Southern agriculture and agriculturalists.

### 3.1 History

The case studies noted above illustrate several important themes, which help to orient how the degrowth movement may better

---

[24]    M. Friant, & J. Langmore, "The Buen Vivir: A Policy to Survive the Anthropocene?" in *Global Policy*, 6:1 (2015): 64-71.

[25]    A. Johnson, "Pudrición del Cogollo and the (Post-)Neoliberal Ecological Fix in Ecuador's Palm Oil Industry" in *Geoforum*, 80 (2017): 13-23.

understand and interact with Global South agriculture and rural spaces. The first is history. It is axiomatic that the Global North has and continues to heavily influence agriculture and rural spaces in the Global South. Notwithstanding, any serious attempt to engage these spaces must begin with unraveling and identifying the complex historical processes influencing them. Two notable places to begin are with colonialism and slavery. Colonial land appropriations drove - and continue to be a root cause of - the highly unequal distribution of land across Latin America and in other areas of the Global South. Coupled with slavery, they formed historically novel land-labour social relations facilitating massive colonial resource extraction from the South. In Ecuador, enslaved African and Afro-descendent people historically worked in the gold mines found in the Northwestern province of the country called Esmeraldas, dating back to the 1500s (Rapoport Center 2009).[26] In current times, palm oil plantations reside in many of these same areas and it is Afro-Ecuadorians who largely fill the menial labor positions in these operations. Despite being seen as a distinct group of peoples (acknowledged in the Constitution), Afro-Ecuadorians continue to be disenfranchised by a lack of representation in environmental institutions and this has contributed to the legal and illegal appropriation of their lands for plantation purposes. Indigenous peoples of Ecuador are also subject to similar experiences due to the entrenchment of marginalizing (and highly racialized) processes in the country's legal framework.

These processes fit into a broader historical logic of global capitalism, which influences Global South agricultural spaces in multiple ways. Neoliberal reforms of global trade have facilitated the opening of formerly protected markets, putting into competition heavily subsidized and mechanized producers from places like the United States with low tech and non-subsidized farmers in the Global South (this point is discussed in greater detail below). At a

---

[26] Rapoport Center, "Forgotten Territories, Unrealized Rights: Rural Afro-Ecuadorians and their Fight for Land, Equality, and Security," University of Texas at Austin Law School (2009).

more localized scale, appropriationism drives the transformation of formerly farmer-controlled activities (e.g. fertilization via animal manures) with industrial processes (e.g. mineral fertilizers).[27] These processes transform peasant and autonomous agriculture into semi-autonomous and increasingly capitalist agriculture, with market competition the main underlying driver of this process. When seen in combination, and in geographically specific ways, they help to explain the geography of agriculturalists and agricultural practices.

It is important to highlight that these transformative processes can be both global in nature (e.g. capitalism), and have geographically-particular manifestations. This recognition can simultaneously serve as a means to draw common cause with social movements acting against generalized neoliberal policies. It can also serve as a means to better integrate how Global North policies and power affect both the policies enacted in the Global South, and the ability of social movements to counteract them. It may also lead to less universal degrowth prescriptions and ones that are more sensitive to the particular needs and socio-ecological geographies and histories of countries in the Global South. Additionally, recognizing the firmly entrenched legacies of colonialism in agricultural institutions complicates suggestions offered by degrowth proponents that degrowth in the North will automatically allow the Global South to pursue its own autonomous forms of development. Furthermore, this recognition illuminates the current ways extraction processes function through enduring racialized, gendered, and class forms and problematizes the simplistic degrowth assumption that countries can easily de-link from deep-seated systems of oppression.

## 3.2 Markets

Trade in agricultural products has been a primary driver of changes in agriculture and rural spaces in the Global South. Analyzing how

---

[27] D. Goodman, B. Sorj, & J. Wilkinson "From Farming to Biotechnology: A Theory of Agro-industrial Development" (1987).

this trade has changed over time, and the changes this trade has engendered helps to foreground Northern-Southern connections, and the evolving ways they continue to co-create specific forms of agriculture and rural spaces. A growing understanding of Northern-Southern linkages via trade can be a starting point for the degrowth movement to engage with the South, and envision meeting points for a collaborative future.

The short vignettes above help to locate particularly noteworthy aspects of how trade reshapes agriculture in the South. The colonial origins of trade, and the violent processes through which Global South peasantries were brought into markets is one important aspect to highlight. The legacies of these early and violent linkages continue to shape the distribution of resources (e.g. land) and the distribution of rewards and risks of agricultural production in the Global South today.

Another important area to consider is the role that Northern agricultural crises play in shaping Southern agriculture. Massive surpluses in agricultural commodities, and declining returns for Northern farmers have led countries such as the United States to seek markets for these surpluses abroad. The view that the Global South could be a 'fix' for Northern agricultural surpluses was further facilitated by the use of food as a geopolitical tool during the Cold War era. Food aid became a way to prop up particularly favorable regimes in geopolitically important areas (e.g. Sudan), while laying the groundwork for the future sale and trade in these same staple commodities, with profound implications for both national food self-sufficiency for Southern countries, and for small farmers.

The opening up of the South via global trade negotiations and conditionality agreements as part of structural adjustment loan packages deepened Northern-led transformations of Southern agriculture. Southern tariffs on Northern agricultural products were dismantled, as were small farmer support programs such as price supports, specialized credit programs, and agricultural extension. New donor-negotiated agricultural policies favored growth in export-oriented agricultural production, leading to new crops being grown (e.g., palm and pineapple). These export oriented crops required capital and knowledge - and generally favored larger enterprises and transnational capital. These also mapped well onto existing unequal land distribution rooted in the colonial era. Staple crop growers in Costa Rica, Ecuador, and in those parts of the South most integrated into global markets, have almost completely lost out, either transitioning to other crops, or leaving agriculture altogether. Those who already specialized in commodities for export, such as in coffee, have also experienced losses as the International Coffee Agreement which essentially sustained high global coffee prices was dismantled in 1989.

But the cracks in the globalized food system are beginning to be exposed, most recently with the global food prices spikes of 2007/2008. The opening of agricultural markets, and the trade in grains has led to considerable dependencies on food importing nations. These dependencies - and the risks associated with them - became apparent when prices of major staple crops, and principally rice - led to a massive increase in global hunger, and spurred social resistance across the South.[28] As a result, many Southern countries have renewed efforts to improve national food self-sufficiency[29], directing state-level resources to the production of nationally important staple crops.[30]

Nonetheless, Global North agriculture continues to produce massive surpluses of major staple crops, which continue to put Northern farmers out of business, and vastly impacts the ability of small scale Southern farmers to sustain themselves. It also stymies national goals of food self-sufficiency. In short, Global North overproduction must

---

[28]    W.G. Moseley, J. Carney, & L. Becker, "Neoliberal Policy, Rural Livelihoods, and Urban Food Security in West Africa: A comparative Study of The Gambia, Côte d'Ivoire, and Mali" in *Proceedings of the National Academy of Sciences*, 107:13 (2010): 5774-5779.

[29]    J. Clapp, "Food self-sufficiency: Making sense of it, and when it makes sense" in *Food Policy*, 66 (2017): 88-96.

[30]    B. Dowd-Uribe, M. Sanon, C. Roncoli, & B. Orlove, "Grounding the Nexus: Examining the Integration of Small-Scale Irrigators into a National Food Security Programme in Burkina Faso" in *Water Alternatives*, 11:2 (2018).

be seen as a primary driver of Southern agriculture transformation and possibilities. So the call by degrowth activists to recognize that a reduction in Northern resources use and consumption will lead to spaces of transformation of the South is important. But degrowth activist attention towards Northern agricultural surpluses - not simply consumptive practices - can further facilitate the opening of space for Southern transformations. This is where a co-created vision for what a small farmer-friendly, localized food system may be a shared and common goal, and a fruitful area of engagement.

## 4. Preliminary concluding remarks

This paper sought to bring attention to how Global North and Global South agriculture and rural landscapes are interlinked, an issue which thus far has been overlooked in the degrowth literature. We forward two themes as a way of understanding these linkages. The first relates to the history of agricultural spaces and how these spaces cannot be divorced from the colonial and racialized institutions of their past and present. Degrowth scholars must seriously consider how such institutions shaped and continue to shape the social and economic relations which set the foundation for contemporary capitalist agriculture. Another linkage relates to the theme of markets. We highlight the dialectical nature of the relationship between agricultural markets of the Global North and South by discussing the profound effects that agricultural surpluses and trade agreements have across the Global South. These themes are just two of many that we see as having growing importance as the degrowth project expands in conceptual and geographical scope. Other relevant topics we see as raising questions for more productive discussions include technology, labor, and land relations. Focusing on these issues in the near future will add important (and much needed) dimensions to degrowth work on agriculture in the Global South.

We further argue that examining the history and market dimensions of agriculture helps to envision ways to decolonize the degrowth movement and enable connectivity to Southern social and environmental movements. Recently, sympathetic critiques have challenged degrowth activists to consider ways to decolonize the movement and to create pathways to engage Southern social and environmental movements.[31] Our brief analysis of North-South linkages in agriculture centers interconnectivity and the globality of a shared struggle. It challenges the dominant framing that "degrowth in the North will liberate ecological space for growth in the South... [and] liberate conceptual space for countries there to find their own trajectories to what they define as the good life"[32] by arguing this simplistic interpretation further reinforces the primacy of Northern actors and incorrectly positions them as the key drivers of change.

Engaging an interconnected agriculture recognizes the enduring colonial arrangements that continue to structure monoculture agriculture in the Global South. It also highlights how these arrangements are imprinted on local social and environmental institutions and power relations making them impossible to escape. An interconnected agriculture also demonstrates that reducing Northern consumption is insufficient to fully open Southern development futures. In other words, the South cannot envision a new path forward without a recognition that Northern surpluses and the forcing open of markets have also profoundly affected past, present, and proposals for more sustainable and just futures in the South.

Our analysis challenges the degrowth movement to stretch beyond a framing of the central problem as one of overconsumption driven by an unbridled capitalism - to one linked more intimately with a transnational (neo)colonialism and power. This subtle but important reposturing of the degrowth movement could open up space to create natural linkages to Northern *and* Southern movements, including as

---

[31]   Escobar, "Degrowth, postdevelopment, and transitions: a preliminary conversation." Nirmal & Rocheleau, "Decolonizing degrowth in the post-development convergence: Questions, experiences, and proposals from two Indigenous territories."

[32]   G. D'alisa, F. Damaria, G. Kallis, Eds., *Degrowth: A Vocabulary for a New Era* (New York; London: Routledge, 2015), 5.

it relates to agriculture, anti-racism, food sovereignty, agroecology, and indigenous movements. It could also pull the degrowth movement into a deeper engagement with Southern social movements to envision and co-create local and global imaginaries for a socially just and environmentally sustainable future. A close analysis of North-South linkages in agricultural and rural spaces may move the degrowth movement one step closer to envisioning these new global engagements.

# Our Common Home and the True Dharma Eye: Dōgen and Laudato si' in the Anthropocene

Gerard Kuperus*

In an era that has – for better or worse – been coined the "Anthropocene," our dominion of the earth has come to its inevitable conclusion: even geologically the earth is now ours. The very name "Anthropocene" suggests a certain sense of ownership and domination. It is a relationship with the land that suggests that we own the land. This "we" is far from inclusive. It is an exclusive "we" that drives out others who are deemed illegal and wipes out species across the globe. Ownership of the land is, I argue, not only a mistake, but as we can see in the examples of xenophobia and extinction, a dangerous idea. Ownership leads to destruction of the land and other species, as well as the oppression of other groups and ultimately us as individuals. Our sense that the land is ours fails to grasp our relational and contextual nature, and how we, in fact, belong to the earth and not the other way around.

* Gerard Kuperus is an associate professor in philosophy at the University of San Francisco. His work focuses on the significance of place and is inspired by both the Western tradition of philosophy as well as Zen Buddhism. He is the author of *Ecopolitical Homelessness: Defining Place* in an Unsettled World (Routledge 2016), the co-editor (with Marjolein Oele) of *Ontologies of Nature* (Springer 2017), and (with Josh Hayes and Brian Treanor) *Philosophy in the American West: A Geography of Thought* (Routledge 2020).

In this essay I specifically reflect upon the Zen-Buddhist tradition (through Dōgen and Gary Snyder) and the encyclical *Laudato si'* by Pope Francis, two sources that in their own terms emphasize the interconnectedness of all. *Laudato si'* emphasizes our lost connection with nature and proposes an integral ecology, in which economic, social, and natural ecologies have a common origin and future. Through the Zen Buddhist tradition we can recognize the land itself, all of nature, as a mind – as a larger rationality in which we are placed. It offers a criticism of Western traditions of thinking often rooted in an independent and unchanging idea of self. This notion of the self, it has been argued, is the cause of all trouble.[1] It leads, among others, to the urge to claim that something is mine. Within the work of Dōgen and Pope Francis' *Laudato si'*, we find articulations of the interconnectedness of all and a contextualized self, both of which help us to challenge our tendency to seek ownership and domination of the land.

## Praising Our Common Home: *Laudato si'*

In the 2015 encyclical *Laudato si'*, Pope Francis asks us to recognize the environmental and social predicament we find ourselves in: the environmental crisis constituted by pollution, climate change, and loss of biodiversity, paired with a social crisis constituted by the decline in the quality of human life, the breakdown of society, and global inequality. The point here is that the environmental crisis is deeply rooted in a social crisis. Hence, "[w]e are faced not with two separate crises, one environmental and the other social, but rather with one complex crisis which is both social and environmental. Strategies for a solution demand an integrated approach to combating poverty, restoring dignity to the excluded, and at the same time protecting

---

[1]    Cf. Walpola Rahula, *What the Buddha Taught* (New York: Grove Press, 1962).

nature."[2] In other words, it is an incredible mistake to regard our current climate crisis as a management issue that we can fix with better technology or better use of the existing technology. A solution to our environmental crisis can only be successful through a change of humanity, an ecological conversion.[3] Francis further argues that politicians have reacted merely with "weak responses."[4] Reading the well-researched document, one should conclude that the tremendous destruction of our common home, inequality, and the empty call to action of our elected officials are an incredible outrage. Even ignoring the ill-informed, and fact-defying policies of Trump, Obama's policies have been a long shot from stopping climate change. The Paris Agreement merely attempted to keep the global average temperature increase to below 2°C (and "to *pursue efforts* to limit the temperature increase to 1.5°C above pre-industrial levels" (Paris Agreement, my emphasis). To "pursue efforts" is not even stating the limit as a clear goal. Thus, it was always unlikely to be met. As we know the USA has withdrawn from the agreement and the other major industrial nations fail to make significant changes.[5] While (interestingly) Nixon was perhaps the most successful president in terms of environmental progress, the fact of the matter is that no president, no policies, and no technological solutions can alter the course we are on. We cannot rely on leadership to make changes for us, we need to, first of all, change who we are. Currently we are focusing on policies and agreements that *hopefully* – not certainly – will reduce – not stop! – climate change. There is an abundance of proposals for technological solutions, varying from solar shields to floating islands. Yet, is any of that a true solution? We can be reminded here of Plato, who in *The Laws* writes about two kinds of medical doctors, a poor kind of doctor

---

2  Pope Francis, *Laudato si': On Care for Our Common Home : Encyclical Letter* (Rome: Libreria Editrice Vaticana, 2015), 104.

3  Ibid, 8 and 157 ff.

4  Ibid, 39 ff.

5  David Victor, Keigo Akimoto, Yoichi Kaya, Mitsutsune Yamaguchi, Danny Cullenward, and Cameron Hepburn, "Prove Paris Was More than Paper Promises," in *Nature News* 548 (7665): 25, 2017.

who only treats symptoms and the truly good doctor who discovers and treats the cause of the illness. In dealing with climate change we seem to be the poor doctors: instead of dealing with the true causes (over-consumption, pollution, over-harvesting, unsustainable use of fossil fuels, etc.) we are merely trying to find solutions for the symptoms of "our decease."

Indeed, Pope Francis makes a similar point when he writes: "There needs to be a distinctive way of looking at things, a way of thinking, policies, an educational programme [sic], a lifestyle and a spirituality which together generate resistance to the assault of the technocratic paradigm. […] To seek only a technical remedy to each environmental problem which comes up is to separate what is in reality interconnected and to mask the true and deepest problems of the global system."[6] In other words, technology alone will not solve the issue. Even more, it will make matters worse, as we keep focusing on the symptoms, not on the causes, which is rooted in our technological relationship to the world. As Jason Wirth puts it "only asking the engineers for a solution is like asking the drunks to run the brewery."[7] We first have to overcome our intoxication and overcome our need to imbibe before we can responsibly run the brewery.

Our intoxication is also directly tied to the great injustice of climate change. Those who run the brewery are for now still fine, while the poor are facing the most immediate effects. As Pope Francis writes: "Climate change is a global problem with grave implications: environmental, social, economic, political […] It represents one of the principal challenges facing humanity in our day. Its worst impact will probably be felt by developing countries in coming decades."[8] One example of this can be seen in the nation of Kiribati, consisting of 32 low-lying atolls and reefs in the Pacific Ocean around the equator.

---

6    Pope Francis, *Laudato si': On Care for Our Common Home : Encyclical Letter* (Rome: Libreria Editrice Vaticana, 2015), 83/4.

7    Jason Wirth, "Philosophy In a Time of Crisis," in: *Extinction Event*, accessed April 4, 2019, https://www.philosophyx.co.uk/wirthextinctionevent.

8    Pope Francis, *Laudato si': On Care for Our Common Home : Encyclical Letter* (Rome: Libreria Editrice Vaticana, 2015), 20.

Historically the equator has been free of tropical storms, but this has changed recently. Rising sea levels combined with these unusual tropical storms threaten the 110,000 inhabitants of Kiribati. It is at this point quite certain that the nation will be completely underwater by the end of the century. They do not have the resources to elevate the islands or build sea walls and so their only option might be to move. Such a change will have destructive effects on their identity given that who they are is strongly connected to the place where they have lived for thousands of years. The nations that formerly colonized places such as Kiribati (in this case the UK) are now completing their destruction of what remains of such indigenous communities.[9] Numerous cultures have been destroyed through the process of colonization. Indigenous cultures have lost their natural resources, their place, and their culture. Climate change is the next step in this colonial development, even touching cultures in some of the remotest areas of the world.

Climate change as a social justice issue also hits on the local level. In the San Francisco Bay Area, low lying geographical areas are already flooding during king tides. It is again the poor (and often people of color) who are hit the worst. For example, in the affluent county of Marin, the public housing area in Marin City only has one road of access. This road floods during king tides, making it impossible to get in or out of the area. There are many options to extend other roads into the area, but this has purposely been avoided, since it would connect the poor area to some wealthy areas. It is to be expected that in the Bay Area, as sea levels rise, wealthy areas will build seawalls and elevate the land. Those mitigations will further increase the problems in other (poor) areas, as water will need to go somewhere.

The examples of Kiribati and poor areas in the San Francisco Bay Area are some of the many examples that convey the urgency as to

---

9    *Anote's Ark* is a documentary on the plight of the people of Kiribati, and the attempts of their president, Anote Tong, to find a solution for their predicament. Matthieu Rytz, Bob Moore, Mila Aung-Thwin, Oana Suteu Kintirian, Anote Tong, Tiemeri Tiare, Patrick Watson, *Anote's Ark*, Documentary Channel (Television network: Canada), 2018.

why a more permanent solution must be sought out. It should be made clear that while initially climate change might predominantly affect the poorest nations and the poorest people – those who contribute the least to climate change – no one will be immune. As Anote Tong, president of Kiribati rightfully says, "What is going to happen to us, is going to be the fate of the rest, who will follow."[10] If it is not water, it will be droughts, fire and smoke, or cold and/or heat that cannot be escaped.

Thus, we have urgent reasons to change the course we are on. Yet, how do we accomplish that? I suggest that we must change our understanding of who we are and take into account Pope Francis' claims that political policies and technological solutions are simply not enough to resolve the current environmental issues that plague our common *home*. All solutions need to come from a different kind of humanity, a humanity that sees itself as part of the earth. We can create more fuel-efficient cars, harvest the energy of the sun, pollute less, or produce greener products, yet they remain merely at the level of the symptoms, not the true cause of the problem. If we do not drive or consume less and live differently, which has to come from a change of who we are, we will not resolve this crisis.

The underlying issue, for Pope Francis, is our humanity, which is lacking the basic insight that we share a common home with all of humanity and all other living creatures, as well as the inanimate world. We are but one part of the earth. This should not come as a big surprise, yet our behavior indicates otherwise. Along these lines Pope Francis asks us to recognize that we are the dust of the earth: "We have forgotten that we ourselves are the dust of the earth (cf. *Gen* 2:7); our very bodies are made up of her elements, we breathe her air and we receive life and refreshment from her waters."[11] The problem needs to be solved at the root: "Many things have to change course, but it is we human beings above all who need to change. We lack an awareness of

---

[10]   Ibid.

[11]   Pope Francis, *Laudato si': On Care for Our Common Home : Encyclical Letter* (Rome: Libreria Editrice Vaticana, 2015), 2/3

our common origin, of our mutual belonging, and of a future to be shared with everyone."[12] Thus, here is the true diagnosis of our sickness: we have lost touch with our home, the earth, as well as with those with whom we share the planet. We have lost ourselves and replaced it with a selfish, self-centered, and consuming self that does not recognize its own destructive behavior and finds answers in temporary solutions.

In order to further explain the idea that we are the dust of the earth, Pope Francis argues that "When we speak of the 'environment,' what we really mean is a relationship existing between nature and the society which lives in it. Nature cannot be regarded as something separate from ourselves or as a mere setting in which we live. We are part of nature, included in it and thus in constant interaction with it."[13] The term "environment" is a problematic concept, since it suggests a certain distance between ourselves and that which environs us. Against such a separation between ourselves and environment, Pope Francis moves in the direction of an integral understanding of ourselves and our environment or nature. We are a part of nature; our environment is not separate from us.

How have we forgotten this simple insight? Pope Francis provides a clear message that there is something utterly wrong with the way we live our lives, wanting more and more, without truly enjoying our lives. We are anxious and those who have the means to do so try to subdue the anxiety through consumption. Francis identifies a sickness in our current way of being, in which consumption is a remedy for our unhappiness. Yet, instead of attacking the true causes of our unhappiness, we (unsuccessfully, or at best temporarily) only address the symptom. Freedom is confused with "freedom to consume."[14] Interestingly, in both climate change and the destruction of the earth, and the curing of our sickness we merely seek temporary solutions, failing to address the deeper causes. Discussing our global world in which selfishness is reigning, he writes: "The emptier a person's

---

12   Ibid, 149
13   Ibid, 104
14   Ibid, 150

heart is, the more he or she needs things to buy, own and consume. It becomes almost impossible to accept the limits imposed by reality. In this horizon, a genuine sense of the common good also disappears."[15] Consumerism leads to an empty identity, since it fulfills needs that have no clear ends. This empty identity creates instability. We react to this by enclosing and centering ourselves. The result of this, as Pope Francis argues, is "[w]hen people become self-centered and self-enclosed, their greed increases."[16]

Treating an illness that is deeply rooted in our very being is complex, to say the least. The solution Pope Francis offers is an ecological conversion in which we become more passionate, develop a concern for the earth in terms of a protection of "God's handiwork" and work as a community, linking us "to all beings."[17] Furthermore, he argues, we should be led by a Catholic spirituality, which he explains as a "less is more" conviction in which simplicity and moderation can lead to a true enjoyment of the small things, as opposed to "the accumulation of pleasures."[18] I will discuss this in more detail in the conclusion, but will now turn to Dōgen's Zen Buddhism, which offers us a more positive outlook on losing ourselves.

## The True Dharma Eye

In his *Mountains and Waters Sutra* (*Sansuikyo*), 13th Zen Master Dōgen (1200-1253), founder of the Soto Zen School, cites a koan of Priest Daokai of Mt. Furong: "The blue mountains are constantly walking" soon followed by Dōgen's insistent phrases to study the walking of mountains, since, "[i]f we doubt the walking of the mountains, we also do not yet know our own walking."[19] *Dōgen here emphasizes the*

---

[15]   Ibid, 150

[16]   Ibid, 150.

[17]   Ibid, 157, 158, 159, 16.

[18]   Ibid, 162

[19]   Dōgen, "The Sutra of Mountains and Waters," In: *Shobogenzo*, Book 1, Gudo Nishijima and Chod Cross (Tr.), (Charleston, SC: BookSurge, 1994), 141, 142

*fluidity of mountains which we typically think of in terms of solid and unmoving. Yet, mountains are the result of extremely powerful geological processes which are far from finished. Sometimes we feel the "walking" of the mountains during earthquakes, through their seasonal changes, rapid changes in the weather, and so forth.* While this might shed some light on the idea that mountains are not static, it still remains puzzling why Dōgen uses the verb "walking." We might suggest it as just a metaphor, yet he insists that "the walking of mountains must be like the walking of humans."[20] This does not only mean that the mountain walks like us, but that we walk like the mountain: we change with the seasons, shake with the mountain during an earthquake, get nourished by the mountains, or the earth, and when we die our bodies return to the mountain. In other words, we are the mountains. To understand ourselves is to understand this intricate relationship. This relationship is expressed in terms of emancipation realization, of being the self in the opening of Dōgen's fascicle:

"The mountains and water of the present are the realization [actualization] of the words of eternal Buddhas. Both [mountains and water] abide in place in the Dharma having realized virtue. Because they are in the state before the kalpa of emptiness they are vigorous activity in the present [they are alive at this moment]. Because they are the self before the sprouting of creation, they are real liberation [they are emancipation realization]."[21]

While we might regard mountains as complete, we do not typically regard that completeness as actualizing the Buddha way or as the path towards some kind of enlightenment. So, why would Dōgen make these suggestions that seem to contradict common sense? Starting with the idea of "actualizing the Buddha way" he refers to the Buddhist insight that enlightenment is not a transcending to some higher realm, but rather an opening up to the world (the Buddha land) that lies right in front of you but had never been recognized before. It is this enlightenment as immanence through which we come to a

---

20    Ibid, 141
21    Ibid, 141

oneness with the world. Notions of self and other are brought into question and as we start to recognize that the mountains are alive and much older than us, we also start to recognize that we are these mountains.

In the *Mountains and Waters Sutra,* Dōgen shows the intricate relationship between water and mountains, often challenging common perceptions. Mountains turn out to be much more fluid, witnessed by the way a powerful body of water creates erosion and carves a river or shapes the seashore. Mountains and waters should be taken as a metaphor for the processes of the earth. It is valuable to consider the work of poet and writer Gary Snyder, who studied Zen in Japan and is greatly influenced by Dōgen. Snyder suggests that Dōgen's " mountains and streams are the processes of this earth, all of existence, process, essence, action, absence; they roll being and nonbeing together. They are what we are, we are what they are."[22]

Pope Francis used the biblical language of the dust of the earth. We are made of the very material of the earth. This insight leads us to consider ourselves as a part of our common home, the earth. Dōgen provides a more radical insight: we are not merely a part of the mountain and rivers, we *are* the mountains and rivers, and the mountains and rivers *are* us. Any kind of distinction or category, linguistic or otherwise, is brought into question. Mountain and river, self and other, mountain and human, all is interrelated in an essential way, in which each and every thing only exists in so far as it is in that relationship.

To further elucidate how this interrelatedness and contextualization is related to the "Anthropocene" let us turn again to Snyder. In his poem "What Happened Here Before" he illustrates, in a few words, our failed relationship to the land by narrating the tremendous history of Northern California, spanning 300 million years. The poem illustrates powerfully the walking mountains as well as "the Anthropocene." Materials such as granite and gold and the mountains and riverbeds

---

[22]     Gary Snyder, *The Practice of the Wild,* (San Francisco: North Point Press, 1990), 103.

in which these materials are found were formed through processes lasting hundreds of millions of years. By contrast, the era of what Snyder calls "the white man" destroyed most of those natural features in just over 150 years. Snyder then asks to whom belongs the land? His answer is astonishingly simple: "the land belongs to itself."[23] He adds, in quotation marks, the Buddhist insight of impermanence "'no self in self: no self in things'" an idea that complicates the boundaries of property and will be touched upon at the end of this section. In the penultimate lines of the poem, situated in between mentions of military jets and a blue jay, Snyder turn us to a powerful yet simple insight regarding human history in the grand scale of things:

WE SHALL SEE
WHO KNOWS
HOW TO BE[24]

Who knows how to be? Snyder lets the reader choose between "[p] onderosa pine, manzanita, black oak, mountain yew, deer, coyote, bluejay, gray squirrel, ground squirrel, fox, blacktail hare, ringtail, bobcat, bear [...h]uman people [...] with basket hats and nets [...] the white man."[25] I should point out that "white man" is not to be taken literally here, but as a metaphor for colonization and what we could call "anthropocenic" forces. "White man" is contrasted with "human people with basket hats and nets" as well as with the animals, vegetation, and the inanimate objects created by long natural processes. The rivers and mountains with all their processes, the land and sea, all know how to be. Indigenous communities found their place in this rationality, yet "white man" brings their own "rationality." Of course, it is outrageous to call the destruction of so-called "primitive" cultures progress, while the "white rationality" leads to the destruction of the very possibility to live on this earth.

---

23   Gary Snyder, "What Happened Here Before," in: *Turtle Island* (New York: New Directions, 1998), 80.
24   Ibid, 81.
25   Ibid, 79.

Snyder's statement "we shall see who knows how to be" invites us to reflect on questions regarding our so-called progress: Have humans become better citizens of the earth? Have we learned anything since the Athenians developed democracy, since the Romans conquered and lost, or since the Europeans colonized the new world and used slavery to build it? The answer is that we fail to "know how to be" since we cannot live without destroying others, the earth, and ultimately ourselves. We do not only fail on a human level (letting human others either literally or metaphorically drown) but we, moreover, fail as citizens of the earth.[26] The failure of human politics can be rephrased within the ignorance of the most basic insight of existence: we are nothing without the community of living and non-living beings that constitute the earth. Those who do not know how to be, fail to recognize this and instead think of the self as an independent entity.

Snyder in his poem captures the nasty history of the United States, as he often does in his work. In particular, the destruction of Native American cultures is prominently present in his work. Turtle Island is a reference to the creation story that we find in numerous North American indigenous cultures. It is, of course, also the title of Snyder's Pulitzer Prize winning book of poetry, on which the poem "What happened here before" is included. The term Turtle Island is a recognition of the wisdom that has been destroyed by the colonial forces that formed the new world. It is also an attempt to rediscover and reinstitute that wisdom, which for Snyder means to re-inhabit the places in which we live. The creation story has many variations. The versions I am familiar with all involve water, mud, and a turtle. Some describe a flood of biblical proportions (note here that the indigenous story is presumed to be much older than the bible) and different

---

[26] I assume that the reader does not need to be convinced of the severity of the environmental crisis we currently face, or that the political in general is in a great crisis. The ease with which we elect people who are not fit for office (or not even vote because we are not truly excited about any candidate) is perhaps an indication of our inability to be responsible political citizens in which we seek to include the views and ideas of others. Why we fail to recognize such an obvious insight is far from obvious.

animals that try to dive deep down to bring some mud to the surface, which is eventually placed on the back of a turtle. The continent that is formed in this process is today known as North America. What is important in this creation story is that different animals work together for the greater good, which is the land, the continent on which these indigenous cultures lived and thrived. This land is thus regarded as the result of a collective endeavor, perhaps even a political process. Instead of a man-like God (noticeably playing a significant role in *Laudato si'*) who uses some words and magic to create the earth in six days, a collection of animals is creating the earth. This is not to say that there is no magic in the Turtle Island story, yet the magic involves elements that are already given (as opposed to being created). In the story, water and earth are most prominently present, in addition to the air or wind and the sun. While in Genesis, God is in complete control of the creation, the animals in Turtle Island lack such complete control. It is a process of trial and error, in which they do hard labor, risk their lives, and sometimes even die, but they are controlled by higher powers. These higher powers are perhaps magical, yet we can translate it in a less spiritual and more down to earth language: the actions of the animals are *informed* by the simple insight that nature is an awe-inspiring power that extends way beyond any human collective.

In his well-known essay the "Rediscovery of Turtle Island" Snyder provides a more theoretical approach to our reconnection to nature. Turtle island is a rediscovery or reinvention of nature in which we ultimately find a "culture of nature."[27] Snyder challenges the idea that nature is the subject of science whereas culture is studied by the humanities. He provides the example of how science attempts to understand the functioning of ecosystems and ways to restore them. While those questions are important, it lacks a more fundamental question, which is why we would want to restore them. "Then to

---

27 Gary Snyder, in David Landis, *At Home on the Earth: Becoming Native to our Place, a Multicultural Anthology* (Berkeley: University of California Press, 2008), 10.

'reinvent nature' could be a creative and constructive task in which we might understand *why* we would hope to recover some of the wild that has been lost or endangered. Then we could begin to lay the groundwork for a 'culture of nature.'"[28] Without first asking the question of why we would restore nature, clear incentives are lacking for those who do not "know" what an ecosystem is "supposed" to be or who simply do not "buy" the story science tells us. In other words, science is not the most essential approach to nature; it can only become essential by engaging with the questions posed by the humanities.

Snyder ultimately tries to ground our own being in nature or ground nature in our being, and with that we start to re-assess our current practices but without being able to provide a good reason why anyone else should care. To say it differently, we recognize that a true restoration of nature is, first of all, a restoration of ourselves and of the human species. It is what Pope Francis asks us to do: cure ourselves. In order to do so, Dōgen provides the basic insight to contextualize ourselves within our place: we are the ecosystem and the ecosystem is who we are. We give up here the separation of culture and nature, redefining what it means to be a human. Along similar lines, Snyder emphasizes that everything is nature and incorporates this notion by using box stores, cars, parking meters, or convenience stores in his writing. Some might attribute this to Snyder's background as an urban beat poet. This is arguably a factor, yet more importantly he wants us to consider all this as part of the world. Within that actual world of beauty and ugliness, Snyder argues for a native inspired ecological renaissance (Snyder 2008, 11). Such a renaissance can partly find inspiration in indigenous traditions, in which cultural festivities, stories and practices have very significant ecological meanings. A culture of nature is not necessarily a return to native or indigenous ways of living, yet it is a way of re-inhabiting the earth – learning to live again.

---

[28]    Ibid, 10

Within this context, Snyder reformulates the pledge of allegiance as follows:

> I pledge allegiance to the soil
> of Turtle Island,
> and to the beings who thereon dwell
> one ecosystem
> in diversity
> under the sun
> With joyful interpenetration for all.[29]

Snyder's pledge of allegiance to Turtle Island can be seen as a way to create a culture of nature. It is a playful and humorous, yet serious engagement with the world and ourselves. It brings up a disturbing history and attempts to redefine us in the most radical way possible. It reflects on the deeply problematic American tradition of pledging allegiance to a flag, to "one Nation, under God, indivisible, with liberty and justice for all." Snyder takes out the flag, replacing it with "the soil of Turtle Island" reflecting the Native American cosmological story. He replaces "Nation" with "ecosystem," the (arbitrary) political with natural process, the wild, or wilderness (where the wild process takes place). He adds the word "diversity:" "One ecosystem in diversity." "God" is replaced by "the sun," with which religion is taken out. Finally, "liberty and justice for all" is now "joyful interpenetration for all."

The idea of "interpenetration for all" brings us back to Dōgen, who declares our notion of self as independent as an utterly mistaken idea. The word "interpenetration" likewise redefines us as interconnected, contextualized beings, challenging the dualism of self and other, and specifically for Snyder between nature and culture. This reinvention of ourselves as nature and developing a culture of nature in which we re-inhabit the earth, starts with a recognition that we are all indigenous to the planet, a simple yet forgotten insight. Perhaps this means creating our own stories – as Terry Temple Williams has

---

[29]    Ibid, 14.

suggested.[30] Snyder's pledge is certainly a way to (re)create our own stories and to reconnect to the soil of the continent that feeds us in so many different ways.

In the poem "What Happened Here Before" we saw this idea that the land belongs to itself, linked to "no self in self, no self in things."[31] Snyder seems to suggest there that the notion of a self leads to an idea of ownership, to domination of what is not the self (the things). As he makes clear, this is not a sustainable attitude; we do not know how to be. We have lost a sense of who we are in relationship to the world around us. The identity and interconnectedness of self and other is lost upon us in the capitalistic economy of machines that kill and destroy. To put it somewhat hyperbolically, we seem to think we live as monads independent from cultural, social, political and natural realities around us.[32] Conversely, we seem to believe that we as selves have either no influence on those other "external" realities, or that the destruction of the planet is somehow not going to have an effect on us. In the spirit of Snyder's thinking, I suggest here that we should "rethink," or more appropriately "rediscover" who we are. Snyder's "knowing how to be" is found in Dōgen's ancient wisdom of mountains and rivers. It is the unity of the earth's processes that we have lost in the politics of "the white man." Snyder's proclamation "we shall see who knows how to be" indicates a certain determinism. His poem's rendering of the history of Northern California suggests that the presence of humans and the destruction of the landscape was inevitable: the discovery of gold had to attract people; likewise, the discovery was a necessary consequence of the formation of gold through incredible and undeniable geological processes. Snyder seems to indicate the irreversible path we follow, a path we are on since we fail to open up to a greater unity with the earth. As Snyder, Dōgen,

---

30  See David Landis, *At Home on the Earth: Becoming Native to our Place, a Multicultural Anthology* (Berkeley: University of California Press, 2008), 122.

31  Gary Snyder, "What Happened Here Before," in: *Turtle Island* (New York: New Directions, 1998), 80.

32  Peter Sloterdijk writes in this way about bubbles.

and Pope Francis suggest, these failures can only be overcome by becoming aware of ourselves as interconnected and as part of a world that itself is rational. We are a tiny part of that larger rationality.

## Conclusion

Pope Francis' *Laudato si'* commands us to change humanity. Dōgen proposes a humanity that lets go a permanent self and that is intertwined with nature. Gary Snyder's "we shall see" comment might indicate that he has given up on humanity, yet within the Zen Buddhist framework he provides, becoming aware of ourselves as a part of the world is an integral part of his thinking. Reading poetry might not seem to be the direct action we seem to need so desperately, yet we have seen how Snyder provides a compelling argument that any research or action can only become essential by addressing the questions asked by the humanities. Poetry and other creative writing can turn us to the "why question" and plant a seed in the form of questions about who we are and what consumerism does to us. Not all hope is lost and I even dare to say that some of those seeds are coming to fruition in powerful ways. Education does play a tremendous role in the planting of these seeds and we see now that the climate marches in Europe and Australia, many organized by youth, are no longer to be ignored. Initiatives such as "The New Green Deal" are by most politicians seen as a threat, yet it is these politicians that lend a hand to the real threat. The youth recognize the threat to their future and the need for a radical change in policies. As Pope Francis writes: "Young people demand change. They wonder how anyone can claim to be building a better future without thinking of the environmental crisis and the sufferings of the excluded."[33] This generation of youth perhaps represents the new humanity that Snyder and Pope Francis ask us to become. Nevertheless, they are fighting an uphill battle, since the rest of the developed world is not ready for this new generation and this new way of thinking. There is a strong urgency to get as many people

---

[33]    Pope Francis 2015, 12.

as possible involved and have conversations about climate change and the need to live differently. Independent of political affiliation, gender, race, ethnicity, class, or nationality, in the long run this will affect all of us.

As Pope Francis puts it: "I urgently appeal, then, for a new dialogue about how we are shaping the future of our planet. We need a conversation which includes everyone, since the environmental challenge we are undergoing, and its human roots, concern and affect us all."[34] He does provide some hints that this dialogue should involve a community of all beings, yet it is Dōgen who tell us to first of all listen to the mountains and waters, for "mountains and waters of themselves become wise persons and sages."

---

[34]   Ibid.

www.ingramcontent.com/pod-product-compliance
Lightning Source LLC
Chambersburg PA
CBHW031523270326
41930CB00006B/499